CAMBRIDGE LIBRARY COLLECTION

Books of enduring scholarly value

History

The books reissued in this series include accounts of historical events and movements by eye-witnesses and contemporaries, as well as landmark studies that assembled significant source materials or developed new historiographical methods. The series includes work in social, political and military history on a wide range of periods and regions, giving modern scholars ready access to influential publications of the past.

John Dunn, Cetywayo and the Three Generals

John Dunn (1834–95) became an infamous figure ('a perfect gorilla') in Britain after his involvement in the Anglo-Zulu war of 1879. A British subject who had lived all his life in South Africa, he spent his early years learning to be an expert hunter of large game before becoming a confidant of the Zulu king Cetshwayo, quickly accumulating wealth and power; although already married, he took forty-nine wives and fathered one hundred and seventeen children. However, when war broke out he sided with the British against his former friend and patron, and was rewarded with a huge tract of territory in the former Zulu kingdom. This book, published in 1886 and edited by his friend D. C. F. Moodie (1838–91), presents his side of the story, and contains fascinating insights into an extraordinary life lived among the Zulus in the nineteenth century.

Cambridge University Press has long been a pioneer in the reissuing of out-of-print titles from its own backlist, producing digital reprints of books that are still sought after by scholars and students but could not be reprinted economically using traditional technology. The Cambridge Library Collection extends this activity to a wider range of books which are still of importance to researchers and professionals, either for the source material they contain, or as landmarks in the history of their academic discipline.

Drawing from the world-renowned collections in the Cambridge University Library, and guided by the advice of experts in each subject area, Cambridge University Press is using state-of-the-art scanning machines in its own Printing House to capture the content of each book selected for inclusion. The files are processed to give a consistently clear, crisp image, and the books finished to the high quality standard for which the Press is recognised around the world. The latest print-on-demand technology ensures that the books will remain available indefinitely, and that orders for single or multiple copies can quickly be supplied.

The Cambridge Library Collection will bring back to life books of enduring scholarly value (including out-of-copyright works originally issued by other publishers) across a wide range of disciplines in the humanities and social sciences and in science and technology.

John Dunn, Cetywayo and the Three Generals

JOHN DUNN
EDITED BY D.C.F. MOODIE

CAMBRIDGE
UNIVERSITY PRESS

CAMBRIDGE UNIVERSITY PRESS

Cambridge, New York, Melbourne, Madrid, Cape Town,
Singapore, São Paolo, Delhi, Tokyo, Mexico City

Published in the United States of America by Cambridge University Press, New York

www.cambridge.org
Information on this title: www.cambridge.org/9781108031387

This edition first published 1886
This digitally printed version 2011

ISBN 978-1-108-03138-7 Paperback

JOHN DUNN,

CETYWAYO,

AND

THE THREE GENERALS.

Edited by D. C. F. MOODIE.

PIETERMARITZBURG, NATAL, MAY, 1886.

Pietermaritzburg:

PRINTED BY THE NATAL PRINTING & PUBLISHING COMPANY
(LIMITED).

MDCCCLXXXVI.

PREFACE.

IT has been stated in a review of the manuscript from which the following pages have been printed that this book will prove of deep interest throughout the English-speaking communities of the world, and a perusal of the work will, I venture to think, confirm such an opinion, as therein will be found important political facts known but to a very few exalted personages ; interesting accounts of Zulu Kings, Chiefs, &c., &c. ; readable tales of hunting, containing many hints useful to the modern hunter ; and many other curious odds and ends, all from the pen of Mr. Dunn, a man in a very unique position.

I must premise by saying that whilst I am now writing Mr. Dunn is fifty or sixty miles away, and the production of the book has been left entirely to me, so that I must apologise to the quiet and retired disposition of the author for giving a slight sketch of him in order to disabuse some of the Home public of the bogie idea they have formed of our Author. Some of the accounts of him in the English papers are very amusing, and he is there described as a perfect gorilla ; whereas in point of fact he is, as I have said, a quiet, retiring, and hospitable gentleman, of pleasant appearance and manners, of good family, and much esteemed by all those who have the privilege of his acquaintance. As will be seen he was much hurt at an early period of his life—when he had lost his father—by being defrauded of his just rights, and he therefore shook the dust off his feet against what we call civilisation, and retired to Zululand, where he simply established himself upon the model of King Solomon, the Wise.

That he was afterwards deeply wronged by being deprived of his country and his chieftainship, after having been of the utmost use to the British cause during the Zulu War, will also appear. But what could he expect of a Liberal Government under Gladstone, who seemed and seem to revel in heartlessly abandoning devoted loyalists, as in the case of the loyal Boers of the Transvaal, General Gordon, and John Dunn, just as Liberal Governments abandoned Poland, Denmark, and, latterly, Greece.

Sir Henry Bulwer, the last Governor here, who, with all his rather ridiculous autocracy, was the—proverbially— hesitant and timid tool of a set of vacillating, invertebrate, weak-kneed and unprincipled political poltroons, whose craven spirit and flaccid attitude has brought our beloved Empire to the verge of ruin, implored John Dunn to stay peacefully on his land near the Tugela in order to act as a buffer between Natal and Zululand, and he would see to his rights. At this time Mr. Dunn, having beaten Sitimela, had the Zulu country at his feet, and a grand career before him. How the promise was kept we have seen.

No wonder that under a Government of this sort Mr. Dunn could not get justice. The headstrong and pernicious sophistry of Mr. Gladstone prompts him—as has been said— to wreck an Empire rather than surrender—not a moral—but a self-evolved principle, and accordingly he has brought Ulster and Home Rule face to face, with sword in hand in the first instance, and dynamite and boycotting in the second.

As far as the fair, fertile, but unfortunate Colony of Natal is concerned, as if she had not enough in hand with her " Bar " at the Durban Harbour and Native and Boer dis- turbances around her, she, in common with other British Colonies, must needs be throttled by the same pernicious influence, proceeding from the heated harangues of a Premier who, it is well known, often erects a superb, elaborate, and most taking structure, upon what he is very well aware is a basis of deliberate falsehood. What the growing Colonies want is home representation, or a *Permanent Colonial Board of Control* in London—something like the Council of India. Their decisions, though not final, would command the attention of the London Press, and thus be forced into public notice. The Premier is against this kind of thing, alleging indirectly, if not directly, that there is a disloyal spirit abroad. Of course this remark is characteristically devoid of that particularity which relates to fact. In 1880 I had the pleasure of caning a Victorian Minister of the Crown in Australia for libelling the Queen in a paper which belonged to him, and the loyalty of the people was strongly evinced by the showers of loyal and congratulatory letters that I received and which —by permission—were afterwards printed. I state it not boastfully, but because the case is peculiarly *apropos.*

It is quite an insular idea—now fortunately being dissipated—that the Colonies are disloyal, and it has been actively kept alive by the wonderful oratory and malevolent, though masterful mendacity, of that high priest of hypocrisy and Ananias of anarchy, Gladstone. Palmerston's saying about the latter gentleman bringing on war and ruin and then stepping into a madhouse is becoming verified. In the meantime it might—in conclusion—be said with Byron,

" E'en Satan's self with thee might dread to dwell,
And in thy skull discern a deeper hell."

The book is perhaps smaller than we calculated upon, but we must bear in mind the celebrated Holkot's remarks upon the evils of a great book—he says "The smallness of the size of a book is always its own commendation, as, on the contrary, the largeness of a book is its own disadvantage as well as a terror to learning. In short, a big book is a scarecrow to the head and pocket of the author, student, buyer, and seller, as well as a harbour of ignorance. Small books seem to pay a deference to the reader's quick and great understanding ; large books to mistrust his capacity, and to confine his time as well as his intellect."

THE EDITOR.

CONTENTS.

CHAPTER XVII.

CHAPTER XVIII.

APPENDIX

JOHN DUNN'S NOTES.

——:·:——

THIS Work was commenced in the Year 1861, and was intended to have been the History of the Zulu Race, combined with a history of my life, my experiences in Zululand since 1858, and my "advice to hunters." In 1878 I was on the point of having all my MSS. published, but seeing the drift of affairs, and noticing that there was every likelihood of a war breaking out, either with the Boers or the Amaswazis and Zulus (I must say that I did not then calculate on a war breaking out between the English and the Zulus), I deferred the publication of them until all was again settled. But in the meantime I was deceived by the Natal Government, so that the Zulu War of 1879 came so unexpectedly upon me that I had not time to get my effects secured. At this time I was staying at Emangete, my place near to the Tugela River, and I sent a messenger to my upper place, Ungoye, to rescue my papers from the approaching Zulus ; but most unfortunately he brought the wrong box, the contents of which were comparatively worthless, whilst the box containing the MSS. was left behind and was consumed in the flames when the Zulus shortly afterwards set fire to the place. This was, of course, a great blow to me, as the studiously gathered and interesting records which I had been carefully collecting for twenty years were thus lost to me for ever, and it is impossible for me to call to mind

A

more than fragments of the contents of the papers thus destroyed. And so perished the results of many a long conversation with old Zulu Chiefs regarding the very origin of their power, and the peculiarities of their customs, &c.

I will, however, endeavour to give, as well as I can, an account of the rise and fall of the Zulu power; but, in this place, by way of a preliminary canter, I must give a short, rough sketch of my life. My father died when I was about fourteen years of age, and my mother when I was about seventeen, after which I took to a wandering existence, having always been fond of my gun and a solitary life. In 1853 I was engaged, as was also my wagon, to go into the Transvaal with a gentleman, since dead, who was then proprietor of a D'Urban paper. On our return, when the time for my honorarium came, I was told I was not of age, and that by Roman-Dutch Law I could not claim the money. This so disgusted me that I determined to desert the haunts of civilization for the haunts of large game in Zululand. I had already had an apprenticeship in the hunting of large game, having often enjoyed this kind of sport with Dr. Taylor, of D'Urban, and the officers of the 27th Regiment, then at D'Urban. We often went out at night to get a shot at the elephants which at that time used to come down on to the flat, where the racecourse now is, and wander all about, often to within a few yards of my father's house at Sea View, near Clairmont. The old house and the gigantic old fig trees have now vanished, and where the elephants then trumpeted, other rushing monsters, called locomotives, now shriek.

Captain Drayson, in his book written some years ago, mentions having met a "white lad" when on the track of elephants in the Berea Bush. This lad was myself. But, telling these tales to the present generation of D'Urban, sitting in comfortable arm-chairs in their well-built houses, will seem like romancing to them. At the time I speak of, D'Urban was nothing but a wilderness of sand heaps, with a few straggling huts called houses.

I started for Zululand in 1853, where I had no fixed place of abode, but wandered about shooting, with varied success, till 1854, when I met Capt. Walmsley, who persuaded me to return to Natal, and take office under him, which I did, and a kind friend he proved to me—more a father than a master. I had not been with him long when luck began to befriend me. Capt. Lucas, the present Magistrate of Alexandra, came through on a hunting trip, and on his return sold me his wagon and oxen for £84. From this time I may date the turn of my luck for good. I exchanged the team of oxen, which was a good one of full grown bullocks, for two teams of unbroken ones. These 1 broke in, and kept on exchanging and selling until I had the good fortune to get together a nice lot of cattle.

In November, 1856, Capt. Walmsley gave me permission to take a short trip up the Tugela River with my hunters in search of Elephants. On reaching Zululand we found the people in a very unsettled state, as it was reported that two of Umpande's sons, Cetywayo and Umbulazi, were preparing to have a fight. My hunters did not like the idea of going on. I, however, persuaded them to do so ; and so we went higher up the Tugela, where we were fortunate enough to bag three Elephants and several Buffaloes. I then decided to return, as the people were all up in arms, and did not sleep at their kraals, as was their custom when fighting was expected. A few days after my return, as an influx of refugees was expected, I was ordered, with the Border Police, to the Tugela Drift (ford), and whilst there Umbulazi, with two of his brothers, came over to beg for some assistance, which the Government, of course, would not give. I, however, got

A2

permission from Capt. Walmsley to volunteer, with any o
the Native Police who might like to go with me. So in on
day I raised a small force and went across the Tugela River
and took up my quarters with Umbulazi's army, which
numbered about 7,000. The second day after my arrival in
camp, the Usutu, as Cetywayo's army was called, came in
sight during the afternoon. As I was scanning the hills
with my telescope, I was the first to see the enemy. On
seeing the great odds against us—the Usutu being about
20,000 strong—I advised Umbulazi to send all the women,
children, and cattle across the Tugela. This he unfortunately
refused to do, and one of his brothers, Mantantasheya, jeered
and said that if I was afraid I might go home, as they were
quite strong enough to cope with the Usutu. This made my
blood boil, as it was not from any fear that I had given the
advice, but with the view of getting the women and cattle
out of our way. I also advised that we should go and meet
the enemy. This, though it was now late in the afternoon,
was agreed to, and our army was summoned and on the move
in a short time. On seeing us advance Cetywayo's army
came to a halt. We then went to within six or seven hundred
yards of the advance scouts, and I fired a couple of shots at
them, which made them retreat, and, it being now nearly sunset,
we also retreated. I must not forget to state that Walmsley's
last words to me as I landed on the Zulu side of the Tugela
river—he having accompanied me in the boat—were, " Make
peace if you can, Dunn, but if you cannot succeed, fight like
devils, and give a good account of yourselves." This I
promised to do.

On the morning of the 2nd of December, 1856, broke
that memorable day. It was a raw, cold, drizzling morning
when the call to arms was sounded. On our army being
assembled, I asked Umbulazi if our scouts knew anything of

the movements of the enemy. The answer was that he did not know. Just then a puff of wind blew his ostrich plume off. This I took to be a bad omen, and so did the warriors, for there was a murmur amongst them. I now had a strong suspicion that an attempt would be made by the enemy to cut us off from the Tugela. I therefore immediately called upon my men to follow me, and rode off towards the river. This was the last I saw of Umbulazi. What I suspected turned out to be true ; and as luck would have it, I rode straight for the head of the right wing of the Usutu that was trying to cut us off. I rode to within about 400 yards, and called out to them to wait for us if they were not cowards, and then galloped back and hastened my small force of about 250, with shields and assegais, and about 40 more men with muskets of every queer variety. Seeing a man on horseback caused a feeling of uneasiness amongst the Usutu, a horse being at that time an object of terror to many of them, and for a time the Usutu remained rooted to the spot on which they stood and where I had left them. As soon as I got my men up— although there must have been ten to one opposed to us—I went straight at them, seeing that that was the only chance of getting out of the now fast-closing circle. Seeing such a small force daring to attack such odds caused a panic amongst the Usutu, as they felt sure that I must be backed up by a very much larger force, and after very little fighting we drove them before us for about half a mile, killing many. I then re-called my men, and although my intentions had been to have only cut my way through, and make for Natal, I now felt confident from the success we had, and being excited, I made up my mind to see the end of it. This was lucky for many of our side, as we had eventually to keep in check the whole of the Usutu army, consequently giving many who would have lagged and got killed a chance of escaping. On

the main road I overtook the jeerer, Mantatasheya, completely
knocked up. He begged me to put him on my horse, but as
his weight was about three times that of mine, and as my
horse had done good work, I did not see it, and so left him. The
French philosopher says that there is always a pleasurable feeling in our breasts when we behold the misfortunes of others ; be
that true or not, generally speaking, in my particular case I
might be pardoned if 1 experienced a momentary feeling of
triumphal satisfaction at his idea of leaving me all the fighting
to do after the jeering way he had spoken when I advised the
retreat of the women and cattle. He had taken no part whatever in the fight.

I tried hard to rally our men—as the Usutu, after the
dressing we had given them, did not press us, but kept following at a respectful distance, merely killing stragglers—but
without the slightest avail. The position was not pleasant,
the Tugela river being in high flood, and I saw that we must
adopt one of two alternatives, i.e., stand and try to beat
them off, or get downward from this point. We began to
overtake and get mixed up with the women, the children, and
the infirm of our party, and in this confused condition we
went on to the banks of the Tugela. I again tried to rally
our men, but without effect. A panic had seized all, and the
scene was a sight never to be forgotten. There were several
traders, with their wagons, encamped on the banks of the
river. They were, of course, obliged to abandon their
wagons, and each man to look after himself. *The faith*
among the Zulus *in the power of a white man in those days
was beyond conception.* (I put these words in italics because
at the beginning of the Zulu War of 1879 the same
faith or fear existed until dissipated by the blundering
vacillation of Lord Chelmsford.) As soon as I got to the
river I was at once rushed at by men, women, and children

begging me to save them. Several poor mothers held out
their babes to me offering them to me as my property if I'
would only save them. And now the Usutu were fairly
amongst us, stabbing right and left without mercy, and re-
gardless of sex, and as I saw that my only chance was to try
and swim for it, I urged my horse into the water, but was no
sooner in than I was besieged from all sides by men clinging
to me, so that my horse was, so to say, completely rooted to
the spot. I now jumped off, stripped myself, all but hat and
shirt, and taking nothing but my gun which I held aloft, and
swam with one hand. Yes, I handed over my horse to a Hotten-
tot and swam for dear life. The ferry boat now crossed towards
me after dodging through a drowning mass of bodies in
a wild and higgledy-piggledy confusion of heads, arms,
and legs, whilst the yelling was something awful. I can
assure my readers that I was deeply thankful when I managed
to climb up on to the boat. The ferryman himself was so
much excited that he hardly knew what he was doing, and
one of my poor fellows who reached the boat with me, and who
was hanging on, he struck over the head, and the man sank
to rise no more. The scene was horrible. The Usutu
were, with terrible earnestness, hard at work with the deadly
assegai, in some cases pinning babes to their mothers' quiver-
ing forms. Having now lost my gun, I tried hard to get
hold of another as I could not stand by inactive and look at
this slaughter ; but although there were several traders there
with their guns in their hands they would not lend me one
for fear that the Usutu might succeed in crossing and then
revenge themselves. Of my small party very few managed
to get across, nearly all of them being stabbed or drowned in
the river. My horse got across all right, and as soon as I could
manage to borrow a pair of trowsers I jumped on him bare
back—without my boots—and galloped off, for I knew that
the report of the fight would cause a panic in Natal. I had

got about half way to the Nonoti—at which place I resided
with Capt. Walmsley—when I met that gentleman, the present Sir Theo. Shepstone, Mr. Williams, the late Magistrate
of Umhlali, and Mr. Jackson, the present Magistrate of the
Umlazi Division of Durban County. These gentlemen were
on their way to the Tugela, as it had been reported to them
that heavy firing had been heard, but they were not aware of
the cause of it.   When I got home I found that owing to an
alarming report that the Usutu were crossing the river, my
Kafirs had started for Natal.   I sent after them, however,
and the messengers overtook them a few miles on their road
to D'Urban.

Cetywayo on this occasion came down to the banks of
the Tugela.   Six of his brothers, including Umbulazi, were
killed on our side.   Cetywayo, in his retreat, swept off all the
traders' cattle, amounting to about 1,000.   After a while,
when everything was quiet again, the Natal Government sent
in Mr. H. F. Fynn (the father of the present Magistrate of
Umsinga) to claim these cattle, but, owing to some mis-
management, he returned without them.

CHAPTER II.

I now approach the subject of my first introduction to
Cetywayo, which led to the position in which I now stand.

From my knowledge of the Zulu Kafir, and from what
I could glean from Natal Kafirs who had been in Zululand at
the time of the fight, I felt sure that I could get back the
cattle of the traders without much difficulty, the only risk
being to myself ; but this I did not think much of, as I was
aware of their character for not harbouring revenge after a battle.   I therefore got permission from Capt. Walmsley—who

did not at all like the idea of my going—and started. I made
a hunting trip a pretext for going, but I was looked upon as
mad, and going to my certain destruction. However, I
started, keeping my destination a secret even from my own
party. I kept with my wagon as far as Eshowe, where I left
it with my hunters to "shoot buffalo," starting, however, for
Pande's kraal, which I reached on the third day. Old Umpande, the father of the late Cetywayo, received me well, and
requested a private interview with me, for he had heard who
I was, and that in the late battle I had helped his deceased
sons. When I explained to him the object of my mission he
seemed rather disappointed, but did not say much then, and
as it was rather late in the evening he told me he would
speak to me the next day. Accordingly, the next morning,
shortly after sunrise, he sent for me and my headman,
Xegwana. He was sitting at the head of the Nodwengo
kraal when we reached him, but as soon as we had seated
ourselves he said, "This is not the place in which I intend to
sit." He then—unaccompanied by his shield-bearer, whose
duty it was to hold the shield over him as an umbrella,
to keep the sun off—walked into the centre of the
cattle kraal, ordering my headman and myself to go with
him. Before he sat down he looked round carefully, bade us
be seated, and then remained silent a while. After which he
said : "Child of Mr. Dunn,—I thought you had come
on other matters when I heard that it was you who died
(metaphorically) with my children ; that is why I said
nothing to you last night. As far as the cattle are concerned
you must go to Cetywayo—they are ready to be given up.
Sifili (the name Mr. Fynn then went by) left them ; I don't
know why, but I can't let you go without speaking what is
in my heart. I must first thank you for the part you took to
help my sons who were being killed. I now thank you with

my mouth, but when all is settled and quiet you must come to me again, and I will give you some cattle as my thanks for what you have done for my children. Although you escaped, I still look on you as having seen their last, but still there is something in my heart I must tell you, and that is that although Cetywayo and Umbulazi fought for my place, I gave the preference to neither. The one in my heart is yet young, and I am afraid to mention who he is, even to you. Of the two that have been killing each other—Cetywayo and Umbulazi —Cetywayo was my favourite, but it was not he whom I intended to take my place. As I said before, he is still too young, but I will send and tell Somseu (Sir Theo. Shepstone). You see I am afraid of letting the sticks of the kraal hear what I am saying." After a long talk, during which he made me give him a full description of the battle—the first true account he had heard—he told me to go to Cetywayo's kraal—Mangweni—about 75 miles down the coast. Xegwana did not like this and told the old King so ; but I said I did not mind, provided he would give me a messenger to go with me. To this the King assented, and told Xegwana not to be afraid, and to me he said, " You are a man, child of Mr. Dunn ; your father was my friend ; try and do your best that no harm comes to my children from them taking the cattle of the whitemen." I promised that if the cattle were restored no further notice would be taken. Next morning I started for the Mangwini Kraal, which I reached on the third day. On my being reported to Cetywayo he immediately sent for me, and, on explaining my mission, he at once said the cattle had been collected, but had been scattered amongst the kraals again, and if I would wait a few days he would have them collected and handed over to me. This fact must be particularly noted, that I was never asked by Umpande or Cetywayo if I had been sent by the Natal Government. Neither did I say upon what authority I had come.

This was my first introduction to Cetywayo.

The next evening I received a letter from Capt. Walmesley, as, not having heard of me since my leaving him, he was getting anxious, and so asked me to let him know all particulars. The next morning Cetywayo sent to me to say I was not to mind what the letter said, and begged me to stay and wait for the cattle. I sent back word to say that I had promised to do so, but said he must have them collected as quickly as he could, as I wanted to get back. On further inquiry I found out that a rumour had got afloat—how, no one knew—that the letter was to recall me, as the troops were coming up, and that I had been ordered to abandon the cattle. I remained two days longer with Cetywayo, and on the third he sent me word to say that the cattle were ready, and sent me messengers to take me to the Ginginhlovo kraal to hand them over to me. He said they were a thousand head. On parting with Cetywayo, he thanked me for staying for the cattle, and said I was to return if the cattle were received all right and then receive some cattle he intended to give me. I got to the Ginginhlovo kraal the next day, and found the cattle all collected to the number of one thousand and one. The odd beast I killed, and started for Natal with the thousand.

I forgot to say that, on leaving Umpande's kraal, I sent two men to my wagon to tell my hunters not to be uneasy and to keep on hunting until I sent for them, so I had only four men left to drive the lot of cattle, which I can assure my readers was a difficult task, as I had to go through miles of country thickly covered with bush. The country I allude to was in the neighbourhood of the Matikulu, between the Ginginhlovo kraal and the Tugela. However, I got down all safe, and with the assistance of a trader whom I found near the

Tugela, and who kindly lent me some men, I got the cattle across the river with the loss of three trampled to death i the struggle out of the steep and muddy bank. On my arrival in Natal I sent to the Secretary of the Traders' Committee informing him of what I had done, and also stating that if he would pay me £250 I would hand the cattle over to him for the benefit of the traders. He wrote back to say that the Government ought to pay me. I then went to Maritzburg, and the present Sir Theophilus Shepstone asked me if I had claimed the cattle in the name of the Government, and on my saying I had not done so, he said "Why not? You must have known that the Zulus were under the impression that your authority was derived from the Government." My answer was that although they might have thought so I had nothing to do with it as long as I succeeded in getting the cattle without committing myself. I further said that, supposing I had said so, and not succeeded in getting the cattle, "Would you not have blamed me for assuming an authority I had not?" The Government, however, ignored my claim, so that I held the cattle until I got the amount I claimed from the traders, which was paid me about two weeks after I got back. I then handed the cattle over, and glad I was to get rid of them, and considering that I had not spent more than two weeks over the job I had made a good "spec."

Shortly after the occurrence of the events above related I went back to Zululand to claim my "present of thanks" from my friend Cetywayo. This I received in the shape of ten fine oxen.

Thus commenced my first acquaintance with Cetywayo. Not long after my second return he sent to me to beg me to go and live with him, as he wanted a "white man as a friend to live near him and advise him." The first message he sent

was by Sintwangu, and subsequently by a man named Umla-
zana, as also by others, all bound on the same errand. I at
first demurred, but afterwards thought on the hardships I had
had to undergo owing to my not being allowed by the Roman
Dutch Law to receive the money I had honestly earned, and the
inducements held out by Cetywayo, including the promise of
land in his country. Considering all this, I say, I made up
my mind to accept his offer and remove to Zululand for good.
When I informed Capt. Walmsley of my determination, he at
first tried to ridicule the idea, but on seeing that I meant
what I said, he tried hard to persuade me not to go, and as an
inducement held out a promise of giving me a title to some
land on his farm Chantilly in Natal, he, poor fellow, forgetting
that he had already told me in confidence that all was mort-
gaged in his father's name. Otherwise I think I might have
been induced not to leave, as I really was sincerely attached
to him, and I believe for the time I was with him, very few
had more control over him than I had. Often in his mad
freaks, still remembered by many Natalians, he would stand
being severely spoken to by me, although he would say
" Dunn, if any other man presumed to speak to me as you do I
would have him out with pistols." To this I used to say, in
a jocular way, " I'm game to argue the point with you with
any weapons you may choose," which style of talk always
brought him round, and he would then slap me on the back
and say " You're the boy for me; let's have something to
drink." Notwithstanding all his eccentricities, he was one of
the most generous-hearted men I ever had anything to do
with. May he rest in peace.

But to proceed. The lung-sickness had broken out
amongst the cattle in Natal, and a law had been passed that
no cattle were to be allowed to cross the Tugela into Zululand. I therefore had to sell all the cattle I had remaining

to me from this disease, and buy a span of young oxen from
a trader in Zululand. These were all unbroken, and a tough
job I had in catching them and breaking them in, and when
I started, it took me six days going a distance of 25 miles,
i.e., to the site of my selected dwelling in Zululand, the
Ungoye forest, which was a part of the country totally uninhabited, and abounding in game. But my main object in
selecting this spot was the advantage of the forest. Cetywayo
himself laughed when he heard which part of the country I
had chosen, and all the people said I would soon leave, as no
cattle would live there, and the wild animals would also soon
drive me away. Sure enough wolves and panthers abounded,
but I had a good pack of dogs, and as I had picked out the
place on account of the forest, and game, I soon made the
panthers and wolves scarce, albeit with the loss of a good dog
now and then. I had now shooting to my heart's content, as
often, whilst building my house, I used to see Buffaloes, and
go off and bag a couple without anyone missing me until they
heard the shots. I was always fond of going by myself, with
sometimes one boy who I used to take with me, more for the
purpose of despatching him for carriers when I shot game
than for anything else. I never liked taking a fellow hunter
with me.

CHAPTER III.

Shortly after I was settled, I got mixed up with the
politics of the country, and was constantly being sent for by
Cetywayo to advise him in any emergency. In 1860, I
started with a friend on a shooting excursion towards St.
Lucia Bay. We arrived there after about a week's trekking
with our wagons. This friend was Lewis Reynolds. The

next day we went out to try our luck and bagged a couple of Koodo and a few other buck. On our return to camp we found messengers from Cetywayo to recall me, as, owing to some unexplained cause, he had got into some misunderstanding with the Natal Government, and there was a fear of invasion from both sides, and troops had been ordered up to the Tugela. So we decided to return, and next morning started back, and kept with our wagons that day, but the day following decided to leave the wagons and ride on to my place at Ungoye, a distance of about 75 miles, which we did. The next day we went on to Cetywayo who was at a new kraal he was building at the Etshowe. On arriving there he received me very coldly, and said that he had not thought that I would have deceived him so soon, and openly said that he was sure I had purposely gone out of the way, as I knew the English were coming in. This I assured him was not the case, and offered to take any message for him to Natal should he really not mean war. On my saying this, his tone began to alter, and he said he had already sent messengers, but he would be glad if I would also go and confirm his words by them. We again saddled our horses, and rode on, doing another good day's journey. Our poor horses now began to feel the effects of the continuous work, and that of Reynolds began to go lame. We, however, got to the Tugela the next morning, and after seeing the Commanding Officer, Major Williamson, of the 85th Regiment, we went on to Captain Walmsley, the Border Agent, and delivered our message, and returned and slept at the camp at the Tugela. The next day, as Reynolds' horse was completely knocked up, we started back home with the remaining one only, riding and walking turn and turn about, until we got to about six miles from my house at Umgoye, when I rode on to order the preparation of some food. On my arrival I waited until about six o'clock in the evening, and as my companion did not put

in an appearance, I sent in search of him, but without any
favourable result, so, thinking that he had got tired and gone
to a kraal, I did not wait dinner any longer for him. Next
morning he turned up. Poor fellow! He had lost his way
in the dark and had passed my place, and, not finding any
kraal, he had passed the night under a rock, cold and hungry.
He was one of the best fellows Natal ever saw. All being
now quiet, we again, after a few day's rest, started back to
the hunting ground, and a good time we had of it, killing no
end of game of all kinds, but as so many books have already
been written on the subject of hunting, I do not intend to
give many hunting tales, with the exception of a few remarkable incidents.

Reynolds saw me shoot my first Rhinoceros. We both
stalked him at the same time from different directions, unknown to each other, but I luckily got up first and fired first.
He, not knowing that the shot came from me, jumped up and
used rather strong language at having his shot spoilt. The
Rhinoceros started off as fast as his legs could carry him, and
we were standing talking (after Reynolds had apologised for
the language used, and explained that he had thought the
interruption had came from a native hunter) when we heard,
some 400 yards off, something like the squeaking of a big pig.
This sound Reynolds had heard before, and he shouted out
" By jove! you've got him—that is his death cry ;" and sure
enough when we reached the spot from whence the sound
came, we found my fine fellow stiff. He was a very fine bull
of the White species. A few days after this I had shot a
couple of Buffalo, and was on the track of another wounded
one, which led me to the bank of the Hluhlue River, where I
saw what I thought to be a Black Rhinoceros, and, not
having shot one, I left the Buffaloes for the new game. On
getting nearer I was surprised to see it was a " Sea-cow " (or

Hippopotamus), an unusual thing to come across, feeding in broad daylight. The spot being rather open, with tufts of grass here and there, I had to go on my hands and knees, and had got up to within about 100 yards of it, when suddenly I came upon an enormous wild Boar (Vlak Vark). He was lying within three yards of me, fast asleep. I did not know what to do. Should I startle him, I would frighten the Sea-cow, and I could not well crawl past him without being seen. Whilst considering what was best to be done, he arose, and immediately saw me, and not knowing what I was, turned to me, champing his tusks. I kept very quiet, but at once cocked my gun, as I expected him to charge me, and I was also strongly tempted to bag him as he had the finest tusks I had seen on a Vlak Vark. In fact I have never since seen such a fine pair, and have often regretted not having got him, as many hundreds of Sea-cows have I killed since. Well, to go on with my pig. He did not keep me long in a fix, for after a few loud snorts and foaming at the mouth he quietly began to turn and edge off. I expect he began to smell that mischief was in store for him. I was in great fear lest the Sea-cow might take the alarm, as it was in sight all the time, but it had either got hold of a nice feed of grass, or else had been fasting, as it looked up twice and went on grazing again as soon as the pig was out of sight. I again crawled on and got to within about 50 yards, and waited until the animal got into such a position that I could give a telling shot. As it was facing landwards, I gave it one barrel behind the left shoulder, and as it turned for its watery home I gave it the second barrel behind the right before it plunged into the river and disappeared. For about ten minutes I sat patiently on the bank, and when it came up in its dying struggle, I fired two more shots into its head, which settled it.

B

When I got back to the camp my companion and the hunters were much surprised to hear that I had shot a Sea-Cow, as that animal had never been found so far up-country in those parts, especially in the daytime.

After having had some very good shooting and bagging between 50 and 60 Buffalo between our party, besides a great number of other game, we struck camp, and returned home. In those days I don't think there was another spot in South Africa where in one day such a variety of game could be met with. Baldwin, the hunter, trader, &c., shot here on his way to the Zambesi, and he, in his book published some time ago, says that, with the exception of Elephants, this was the finest spot in South Africa for game, and even in these days very good shooting is to be got there, although not to be compared with that of the days I am now writing about.

Whilst on the subject of shooting I might as well give a little friendly advice to intending sportsmen. Don't mind expending ammunition before you start on your hunting trip, for then you will thoroughly try your gun and know it well. As a rule the charge put into the cartridges by the gun-makers is too feeble, and the bullet does not penetrate the large game. The best way is to load the cartridges yourself and then you will see the effect beforehand. In saying all this I speak from experience, and will mention an instance in proof. The first breechloader I ordered from England was a double-barrelled one—rifle and smooth bore—the former 16, the latter 12. The charge of powder measured out by the maker for the rifle barrel was 2½ drams—that of the smooth barrel was not regulated, as it was supposed to be intended for shot and small game. My gun arrived on the eve of my starting on a shooting trip, and I made up my mind to do wonders with it. On the way to the hunting ground I loaded

it according to the gunmaker's instructions, and the effect
was pretty good on small buck, but I was surprised at finding
that the bullet had not gone through those that I had shot.
On getting amongst the large game I wasted no end of
ammunition, and only killed a Koodo and a Waterbuck. As
for Rhinoceros and Buffalo, they did not seem to feel the
charge. I was naturally disgusted—especially as one day the
matter nearly cost me my life. Just on leaving camp early
one morning, I espied a large Buffalo bull returning to
cover from the pasturage. I ran and squatted down in the
track he was taking to the bush, and let him come to within
about 20 yards, when I gave a slight whistle, and, as he raised
his head I fired at his chest. With a properly loaded cartridge
the shot would have killed him even if he had not dropped on
the spot. He at once charged straight at me. I rolled on
one side, and he passed ; I jumped up and put in another
cartridge, and followed his blood track, expecting to come
upon him every minute. But he had vanished. This so much
disgusted me that I determined to load some cartridges with
my own charge, even if I spoilt the gun in doing so. So I
returned to camp and loaded a lot with $3\frac{1}{2}$ drams in the 16
(rifle) and 5 drams in the 12 (smooth) bore, and again went
out. After firing a few shots I soon found out that my gun
threw its shots much higher, and that it kicked me, which it
had not done before. But I had my reward, as on coming
across Rhinoceros I killed three, and out of a herd of Buffalo
I killed two, making altogether a bag of three Rhinoceros,
two Buffalo, two Koodo, and one Waterbuck, all on the same
day. In the evening I reached the camp well pleased, but
rather sore in the shoulder from the kicking of the gun. The
next day I bagged five Rhinoceros, and soon got used to the
kicking of the gun. In fact, I found that by grasping it more
firmly whilst firing, it hardly hurt at all. On these grounds
B2

I say that I advise anyone who does not know his gun, to try it well with different charges before he starts on a hunting trip in search of large game.

The behaviour of the Snider rifle is the only thing that is, perhaps an exception to the efficacy of my theory regarding heavy charges. One season I started on a shooting tour with two officers—Captains Carey and Webster. Whilst shooting at a Sea Cow from our boat, the heavy charges of powder that I was using in conjunction with hardened bullets, caused the catch of my gun to fly off, and if I had not had a firm grip of the barrels they would have sprung into the water and been lost. Well, the only other spare gun was a long Snider rifle at the camp which used to throw very high; but not wishing to detain my friends, I sent my gun to the gunmaker in D'Urban, and knocked the back sight off the Snider and took to it for a makeshift, not thinking that I would be able to kill anything but small game with the small charge with which that rifle is loaded. The accident to my gun happened at the Umhlatuzi, a few miles beyond Port Durnford, and we now started for St. Lucia Bay. I had told my messenger to hasten with the gun, and begged the gunsmith to send him back as soon as possible. On arriving at the juncture of St. Lucia and the Umfolozi, I launched our boat and went to give Carey and Webster some shooting at the Sea Cow. We had not been long on the water before we saw one, and rowing within shot, I told Carey to fire, which he did, but missed. On the Sea Cow rising again I could not resist, but fired. I heard my shot tell, but saw the bullet strike the water some distance beyond. Both my friends said I had missed. I said I had not. And for a while we saw no more of the animal, but on going a little distance, and looking back to where I had fired, I saw him floating. (In order that it may not appear paradoxical, I must explain that in

alluding to a Sea *Cow* as " him " I use the generic term
" Sea Cow " by which this animal is spoken of in South
Africa.) On taking him to land, we found the bullet had
gone right through the top of his head. This, as I said, is
an exception to my theory of the efficacy of heavy charges
and hardened bullets. However, my gun got back from
D'Urban a day or two after, and putting away the Snider,
I took it into use again.

On another occasion I was shooting with a rifle presented to me by a young friend of the Hon'ble Guy Dawney's.
It was a peculiar one, made by Holland, and taking the
Snider cartridge. It used to carry very accurately, and I
used to kill a lot of Koodo, Wildebeest (Gnu), and such
game, but I never used to take it out for Rhinoceros or
Buffalo. One day I had been shooting Wildebeest, and
had just killed one, on which I was sitting—my horse feeding under saddle close by—I heard several shots, the sports-
man evidently coming nearer and nearer, when all of a sudden,
about six hundred yards away, I saw one of our party approaching rapidly, galloping alongside of two Rhinoceros, and
firing as quickly as he could. I immediately jumped up on
my horse and rode for him, and then kept turning the beasts
in order to give my friend good shots at them. At last, as
the game did not seem to slacken in speed, and as my horse
was the fastest, I galloped past them, for they were leading
us a long way from the game I had killed, as also from the
camp. I jumped off my horse, and, as the foremost came on,
I fired at her, taking aim between the neck and shoulders,
with the intention of turning her (it was a large cow, with a
half-grown calf.) As soon as the bullet struck, the blood
burst out of her nostrils, and running about ten yards, she
dropped. My friend still stuck to the others. On examining
the Rhinoceros on the side that was uppermost, I could not

find a single bullet wound, and so I thought my friend might
have hit her on the side she was lying on, but on his return
—not having killed the one he had galloped after—we got
assistance from a kraal and turned the animal over, and, much
to his disgust, we could not find a single shot of his—the only
wound being mine—although he had fired at least six or
eight times at her.   This was the second instance of the pene-
trating power of the Snider cartridge.   After this I had more
confidence, and killed many a Sea Cow with the same rifle ;
but these cases, as I have before said, are the exceptions.
The great secret in hunting is to know what your gun can do,
and to shoot straight, with plenty of powder to drive the ball
home.   You must also know the vital spot, and place your
lead there.

    If the above tale of the Rhinoceros ever reaches the eyes
of my friend, he will be amused at the recollection of having
missed the animal.   Whilst relating the incidents of this trip,
I may as well mention an adventure one of our party had
which nearly cost him his life.   I refer to a Capt. Watson of
the 11th Regiment.   I had constantly been warning my
companions not to go about alone, saying that if they would
persist in doing so one of them would get chawed up by a
Lion.   Well, one day we shifted camp to be nearer good
ground for game.   On nearing the fresh hunting ground
the Captain turned off to a mound to scan the neighbourhood
with his glass.   Lying at the edge of a ravine he saw what
he took to be some Impala bucks some four hundred yards off.
Tying his horse to a tree, he crept down into the ravine, out
of sight, and then stalked his game up it, when he suddenly
came face to face with, not harmless Impalas, but about
twenty Lions.   A good shot would have bagged a couple, if
not more, but Watson was none of the best of shots, and,
besides, had a rifle which did not carry true.   He fired, and,

as he thought, gave the finest Lion a mortal shot, the rest moving quietly off, Watson following and firing at them until he had expended all his cartridges but the two with which his gun was loaded, not having, however, wounded any other. He now went back to where he had left the Lion, to see if it wanted settling. On reaching the spot he could not see anything of his quarry until, suddenly, he heard a growl in the long grass close beside him, and at the same instant the Lion sprang at him. He was, at this moment, standing on the edge of the ravine on a bank about ten feet high, overhanging a large pond of water about fifteen feet wide. As the Lion sprang at him Watson had just time to fire both barrels—the cocks of which he had carefully drawn over—and at the same instant jumped backwards, over the bank, into the water-hole, with the Lion on top of him. The brute now caught hold of him, with his mouth, on his side, clawing him on the head with his paw, but the water being deep, the Lion could not get a footing, which fact was the saving of Watson's life, as every time the beast tried to make a firmer bite at him, he ducked himself, as well as his victim, under water, thus swimming about with him as a dog would with a duck, the banks being too high for the Lion to climb out with him. This game went on for some time, which must have seemed an age to a man in the fix described. At last the brute let him go, and swam a little distance off and got out on to a small bank in the ravine. He there sat growling and watching Watson, who by this time had been nearly drowned and was very weak from loss of blood, but he had just strength enough to swim to the opposite bank and catch hold of a branch that was hanging down the bank, and clamber out and make for his horse.

In the meantime we had gone on and pitched camp, and I had gone out and shot a Wildebeest out of a herd that was

grazing about a mile off. I was just cutting off its tail—
(the custom of all hunters, as a display of the tail is a proof of
their prowess), when I saw a Kafir running towards me
and calling out to me to come quickly. I started off running
to him, as I made sure something serious must have happened,
and when I met him the first words were " the whiteman has
been killed by a lion." Well—said I to myself—here is a
pretty mess, it has happened just as I told them. When I
got to camp there, sure enough, was Watson lying in the
tent, and his companions standing around, not one of them,
however, knowing what to do, and afraid to touch him. He was
a pretty sight. His clothes all wet, torn, and bloody—his head
cut open from the back to the eyebrow—like a splendid sabre
cut—and his black beard one mass of clotted blood. I at
once stripped him and washed his wounds with warm water—
cut his hair and bandaged him up. He had a wound on his
side through which the lung could be seen, and smaller
wounds all over his body, but the most remarkable wound
was a welt, or whale, from the middle of his back to near the
large open wound. I could not understand how he could have
got this, as it looked exactly as if it had been caused by a
blow from a heavy stick of the thickness of one's wrist. This
wound turned out to be the most dangerous of all. I was not
afraid of the open flesh wounds, and the one on his head was
only a scalp wound. But I did my best to make him more
easy, and then got a description of the place where the en-
counter occurred. The next morning we started in search of
his gun and hat, and, from what he said, we expected to find
the Lion dead. We found the Lion, sure enough, not dead,
but very savage. We killed him and found that Watson's
shots had done very little damage. His first shot had merely
broken the lion's hind leg, low down, just above the paw.
The shots he fired as the brute sprang upon him had resulted
in the breaking of one of the fangs. The welt across the back

was thus accounted for, as it had evidently been caused by the broken tooth. This breaking of the tooth saved his life, because if it had not been broken and gone in at his back it must have killed him. On looking about we found his gun, and his hat on the top of it, as if carefully placed there, and the Lion's tooth not a yard from the muzzle of the gun, showing how close he must have been.

This escape of Watson's is the most wonderful one I have ever heard of. I forgot to say that whilst looking for Watson's gun we came across the skeleton of a crocodile which plainly showed that the pool was infested by that reptile—so that the triple escape from the Lion, from drowning, and from the Crocodile, may well be described as extraordinary.

We had to wait about a month in this camp before Watson was strong enough to move again. However, not a day passed without our getting plenty of game, and, as good luck would have it for Watson, when he had barely strength to handle a gun, one day, while we were all away from camp, a Rhinoceros trotted up to within about fifty yards of it, and Watson, who always had his gun by his side, managed to crawl to the tent-door and shoot it. He was so pleased at this, that I believe it helped to bring him round more than anything. What used greatly to delight him was to sit under a tree and look at the skin of his Lion, which was a very fine black-maned one. I had it hung up in a tree before his tent. I thought this would be a lesson to the others not to go about wandering by themselves, though I was mistaken, but luckily we had no more accidents, although my friend, Dawney— from what I could make out from the native gun-carriers who used to go with him—had a couple of narrow squeaks from Rhinoceros, but he was a capital shot and a plucky hunter. I often look back to those days, though dangerous, they were the happiest of my life.

The finest bag I ever made was—one morning before ten o'clock—twenty-three Sea Cows. One would think that, with all these carcases, there would be great waste, but not a bit was lost. The natives around St. Lucia Bay used to come down in hundreds and carry every particle of meat away. I shot well that day. I took out thirty-six cartridges, and two in my gun. I brought back six, and two in my gun—killing the twenty-three with thirty shots. That season I killed to my own gun two hundred and three Sea Cows, besides a lot of other game, and was only away for under three months from the day of starting. Colonel Tower and Captain Chaplin were with me that year, the one in which the horse " Hermit " won at home. Sea Cow shooting from a boat is capital sport, as there is just sufficient danger to make it excitable, and the hunter must be very quick in shooting, as the animal shows his head above water only for a very short time. From land it is comparatively tame sport.

Whilst away shooting I constantly received messages from Cetywayo, and on my return he always used to bully me for running the risk of being killed by game.

CHAPTER IV.

Upon Um'Pande's death, in 1872, I discontinued my long hunting trips. Cetywayo had succeeded his father. Previous to this time he had not troubled me much, only occasionally sending for me when he wished to consult me on any important subject. On one of these occasions he had all his headmen with him at the Mangweni Kraal. (This was before he was made King.) On my arrival he told me he intended to send out an *impi* (army) to some petty tribe in the Swazi country. At this time there was a great division

in the Zulu country. Uhamu being the favourite in all the
upper parts, and it was said that Usibepu would side with
him in the event of an outbreak. I, knowing this, as also the
feeling of Cetywayo's own party on the subject, strongly dis-
sauded him from taking such a step as he contemplated. He,
however, held out, and said he was determined to send forth
his impi. Had I followed my first inclination, and not thought
of the future, I should have liked nothing better than to have
joined an impi, but as I had made up my mind to make the
Zulu country my home, and as I should have been a great
sufferer by any defeat Cetywayo might sustain, I made up
my mind to do my best to dissuade him from taking the
course he intended. After failing in all arguments, I told
him to recollect that all tribes out of Zululand were now
armed with guns, and that he must remember what the few
guns I had had at the battle of Undondakusuka (fought
between him and his brothsr Umbulazi in 1856, as I have
related) did, and that he knew that he had not the whole
Zulu nation on his side, but only a small portion, and that if
he suffered the slightest defeat the whole country would turn
on him, and that I would also suffer. I said, "Wait until
you also have guns." After a while I could see that my
arguments began to tell on him. "But," said he, "where
am I to get guns? The Natal Government will not let
people bring them into my country, and you won't help me."
I answered that if he would put off sending his impi out, I
would try what I could do, and I would go to Natal and see
the Governor. This promise gained my point. The next
day I started back home, and a day or two afterwards started
for D'Urban. On my arrival I luckily found the then
Governor, Mr. Keate, and the present Sir Theo. Shepstone,
at the Royal Hotel, where I also put up. I went at once to
Mr. Shepstone (as he was then) and told him plainly the

position I had taken in Zululand, and that it was my object
to arm Cetywayo's party as strongly as I could, because I
believed that in so doing it would be the cause of preventing
another civil war in Zululand, as, if it was known that Cetywayo had guns, he would soon get all the nation on his side
Mr. Shepstone advised me to go straight to the Governor and
state my views to him—he himself did not think I was far
out.   Mr. Shepstone then went and saw the Governor, and
after a short absence returned and told me to go in to His
Excellency.   By his look I was encouraged to state my case
plainly, which I did, and concluded by saying that as I did
not wish to smuggle, 1 would take it as a great favour if His
Excellency would grant me a permit, on behalf of Cetywayo,
to purchase 150 guns, and ammunition for them.   This, after
consideration, he promised to do, and afterwards carried out.
On a subsequent occasion he also granted me another permit
to purchase 100 more guns and necessary ammunition, but
owing to the people of Natal taking up and opposing the
course pursued, I was requested not to make any more applications, which 1 refrained from doing, and as the Government
had acted very liberally towards me, I determined not to
smuggle any guns or ammunition through Natal—a resolution
I stuck to, although often tempted to break it, as many influential people offered me guns, &c., at low prices.

On my return to Cetywayo, with the guns and powder,
he was greatly delighted, and said he now really saw that 1
was his friend, and was advising him for the best.   When I
went on the trip during which Watson was mauled by the
Lion, Cetywayo gave me a number of young men to take
with me in order that I might teach them to shoot.   Some of
them went with me when we started to search for the Lion,
which, when killed, they ate every particle of.   He was very
fat, and Dawney and his friend also tried some of the meat,
which they said was not bad.   I hope my readers will not go

away with the idea that the Lion was eaten raw, for a large fire was made, and all was well roasted first.

Being now in good favour, and no more being said about the impi going out, I tried to carry out a scheme I had in view, *videlicet* that of getting a further grant of land on the Tugela, which was totally uninhabited. This was a belt of country lying between the Tugela and Matikulu Rivers. After a time I succeeded, and upon this fact becoming known amongst a lot of Natal Kafirs—who had been attached to me whilst I was residing in Natal—a number got permission from the Natal Government to come across the border and reside with me. This I also got Cetywayo's consent to and was the commencement of my starting an independent tribe, acknowledging me as their chief and head. Any Natives leaving their headmen or chiefs in Zululand, and coming to reside in the district over which I was chief, were looked upon as having left the Zulu Country, and the King's service, and they were not subject to the King's call to arms, unless under me, and they were as free from allegiance to their former master as Zulus who had crossed into Natal, but, they were not allowed to remove their cattle, which were considered to be forfeited to the King. This those inclined to me did not mind, as long as they were permitted to come under my protection, although many a squabble I had to prevent my people being taken away and killed—life was held very cheap in Zululand in those days, and if Cetywayo has, in some future day, to give an account of all the lives he has taken in cold blood, he will have a heavy score to settle.

The object I then had in view was to try to get the whole of the district (which was sparsely populated by the Zulus) from the Tugela to beyond the Ungoye, under me. I had succeeded, so far, in obtaining both ends, and intended gradually to try and populate the middle district, and to get a title

from the King and Zulu Nation to a strip all along the coast
and the Tugela, to be, as I have said, under me as an independent chief, and being a favourite of the people, I knew
that many a Zulu who had got into trouble with his own
people, would come to me for protection, thinking nothing, as
stated, of the loss of his cattle, owing to the knowledge of
the fact that I would never let a child starve for want of milk
if I had any cattle. My position had now become one of
some consequence in the Country, and I was looked on as
being second to Cetywayo in authority—the poor old King
Pande only holding a nominal position. I now began to feel
a difference, as I no longer had the free and easy time I had
had of it before, but had constantly to receive some big man
as a visitor—Cetywayo's brothers included —and I was now
more frequently sent for by Cetywayo. On one of the occasions on which I went to him he was at one of the Ondini
Kraals. On my arrival he said Somseu (Mr. Shepstone) was
at Nodwengo, and had sent for him, and he wished to know
why ? On my saying this was the first I had heard of it, he
said he thought I would have heard why he had been sent for,
and after a long talk, we separated, and I turned in. Whilst
lying in the hut that had been assigned to me, a little before
daybreak I heard someone asking " Where is the hut John
Dunn is sleeping in ? " I jumped up quickly and got hold
of my gun, and crept to the sliding wicker-work that forms
the covering of the low door, which I quietly pushed aside,
and looked out. Presently I heard Cetywayo's voice calling
to me, and on my answering, he said, " Come out—I want to
speak to you." On my going out he said, " I have not slept
the whole night. My head has been thinking why Somseu sent
for me. I wish you to go ahead before I see him, I will follow,
and you can tell him I am coming, but send me back word
should you see anything wrong." I knew what he meant.

As I had left word at home that I should be back the next day, having just inoculated a lot of cattle I had got from Cetywayo, I sent word home about looking after these cattle during my absence as I could not say when I should be back, and as soon as it was light I started for Nodwengo. On my arrival there I delivered my message, which Mr. Shepstone was glad to get. The next day Cetywayo arrived, and the one following he had an interview with Mr. Shepstone, and returned to the kraal he was staying at. I did not return until late in the afternoon. On my arrival I found Cetywayo in a very bad temper, and talking a great deal. As soon as I sat down, he spoke to me and said, "Does Somseu know about the way his Induna, Ungoza, is going on? Walking about the King's Kraal as if it was his own, and even going into the Isigohlo (the Harem). What does he think he is? What is he but a dog? If it was not from fear of the ' White House ' I would kill him at once." When I spoke to some of Cetywayo's men about this. I found that it was true, and that Ungoza was presuming too much, and making himself too big a man.

On going to Mr. Shepstone's camp the next day, I mentioned this, and advised him to caution Ungoza, or else he would get into trouble. Mr. Shepstone thanked me for telling him.

After waiting at Nodwengo a couple of days for the headmen, who did not arrive, the meeting was put off, and seeing nothing to detain me, and as I was anxious to get back to look after my inocculated cattle, to which Cetywayo did not object, I returned home. A day or two after my departure the meeting between Mr. Shepstone and Cetywayo took place, which meeting, according to all accounts, was rather a stormy one, owing to Cetywayo speaking so strongly on the actions of Ungoza, but with no disrespect or danger to

Mr. Shepstone. Much to my surprise, I heard some years
afterwards that Mr. Shepstone had stated that his life had
been threatened, and that, knowing of the danger, I had left
without warning him. If I had seen any necessity for remaining, or if Mr. Shepstone had thrown out the slightest
hint that he wished or expected me to remain to the last, I
would willingly have done so, even at the sacrifice of my private
affairs. I was warned and told to be on my guard, as Mr.
Shepstone was one of my bitterest enemies. This I heard
confirmed lately by one who ought to know well. The above
shows how one's actions can be misrepresented by one who
should know better, and how easily one makes enemies without just cause. At the same time, Mr. Shepstone has never
said an indignant word to me on the subject, but, on the contrary, whenever he met me he always professed a friendly and
fatherly spirit, and always expressed his pleasure at my getting
on. As far as I am concerned, I can assert that, at the interview with Cetywayo, there was no knowledge of danger, or
intention on my part to leave him in hostile hands, but my
action was simply ruled by my domestic affairs. I am certain
there was no danger, as I knew Cetywayo's aim, at the time
I am writing of, was to keep on good terms with the English
Government, and it was nothing but the conduct of Ungoza
which exasperated him and made him speak in the way he
did, as intrusion into the harem by a common-born man like
Ungoza was a flagrant violation of Zulu etiquette.

It was many years after this time that Cetywayo's feelings towards the English began to change, and the fault lay
with the Government, and the messengers they sent, assuming
a tone of authority he did not recognise. This feeling was
also fanned, at first, by a light breeze from the late Bishop
Colenso, and that breeze eventually broke into a whirlwind,
which ruined the Zulu nation.

I now had to do all Cetywayo's correspondence, and no messenger was sent to the Natal Government without his first consulting me, and when the Natal messengers returned, I had to write the letter. I always heard the verbal message, and read the answer from the Government.

CHAPTER V.

Thus matters went on until Umpande's death, in 1872. Some time after this Cetywayo requested me to go with a deputation to the Natal Government at Pietermaritzburg, and ask that Mr. Shepstone might be sent to represent the English Government, at his installation as King. This request was acceded to by the Government, and in July, 1873, preparations were made to go up to the Amathlabatini, where Panda died, Cetywayo being at his kraal Ondini, near the coast, and eight miles from the former place.

At the time of starting my eldest son was taken dangerously ill, and I was called home where I daily received messengers from Cetywayo. Eventually he put off going to Amathlabatini, as he said he would not go without me. His principal reason for this was that some mischief-makers had been spreading a report that his late rival Umbulazi had not been killed in the fight, but had escaped to Natal, and that now Pande was dead, it was the intention of the Government to make Umbulazi King instead of him. Hence his saying he would not go without me, as he wanted my advice and assistance in the emergency. On my riding over to him one day and telling him it would be impossible for me to leave home, as I daily expected my son to die, he really burst into tears, and said " If you can't go, I will not, the Spirits would not be with me if you did not go." He, however, sent

C

his principal Doctor, and the next day, much to my surprise, two of his *incekus*, or household servants, came with a large black ox. They had orders to sacrifice this animal in order to appease the Spirits, and thus beg of them to allow me to go up. I told them that I did not believe in this, and would have nothing to do with it. But the men said that, whether I liked it or not, they must obey their orders, and, before stabbing the ox, they went through a lot of incantations and exhortations. Although I had often listened to their sermons at their own kraal, I had never been so impressed as I was now with what was said. It was quite a prayer. Strange to say—whether he was carried away by the excitement or the novelty of the thing or not—but my boy, who had hardly been able to move in bed without help, much less to rise up, begged to be lifted out of bed, and, with help, walked to the door to witness the ceremony, and smiled as he looked on— the first time he had done so for a couple of weeks. I can assure you, reader, it had a strange effect upon me. You can laugh at the superstition, but an incident of this kind goes a long way with the Zulus. Further on I will relate another incident of this kind that happened, to my knowledge, some two years afterwards. Shortly after this my son began to show signs of getting better, and I was able to return to Cetwayo, and we then made a start. The muster was a grand sight, thousands on thousands of plumed warriors with women and boys—the two latter being the commissariat train. I was in charge of, and driving his carriage, one I had bought for him. It was the best in D'Urban at the time, and a fine trap. I had four of my own horses in, all greys. I was afterwards sorry I had promised to take charge of the trap as I lost all the sport, but it was Cetywayo's wish to go in the carriage, and he would not trust himself to anyone but me. But it subsequently turned out that he had been per-

suaded by the Indunas not to go in the carriage, as they were
afraid I might serve them the same as I did upon our journey
to the Mangwini kraal, and leave them behind, so their argument was urgent, more especially as the rumour had got
afloat that Umbulazi was coming with Mr. Shepstone, and
that therefore Cetywayo required extra looking after. After
starting and proceeding about a mile, the commencement of
a grand hunt was made and the whole of the following was
thrown out to form an immense circle of about five miles in
diameter, taking in the site appointed for our camping
ground, to which I drove as fast as I could, as getting
through the crowd of followers was a very difficult task. As
soon as I had unharnessed my horses, I took my gun and
made for a good position, but the country was so swarming
with people (as well as with game) that although I had many
a good chance of a shot, I was afraid to fire in case I might
hit someone, especially as, as usual, they closed in with a rush
at the termination of a hunt of this sort. The slaughter of
game was great, and since this hunt, which took place in the
Umhlatuzi valley, the game has been very scarce here. So
many bucks were killed that they sufficed for the food of the
vast concourse, and Cetywayo had no occasion to give his
followers any cattle to kill. Only two beasts were served out
that evening, one for his brothers and one for myself. My
own men had also killed a lot of game. We had a severe
thunderstorm that night—a most unusual thing at that time
of the year—which drenched us all. The morning was fine,
and a start was made in the same order. Cetywayo
announced his intention of walking a certain distance this
morning, and then of getting into the carriage. So I drove
on to where he said he would get in, and, on arriving there,
left the trap in charge of a boy, and went to try and get a
shot, but again the same drawback occurred ; no sooner did a
c2

buck shew itself than there were a dozen heads in a line with
him. At the foot of Inkwenkwe hill, as Cetywayo was
coming up, a fine Bush Buck came running towards me, but
I no sooner made towards him than there was a general rush
for him. This turned him towards Cetywayo, and one of his
Incekus, making a good shot with an assegai, bowled him
over within ten yards of his Chief. Just as Cetywayo got in
sight of the carriage, the horses, for some reason, took fright
and swerving round, broke the pole. I was not in view at
the time, and a boy came running from Cetywayo to tell me.
On getting there I found a pretty mess, but with the help of
some bush-wood I made a splice of the pole. Cetywayo had
in the meantime gone on, and, on my overtaking him, I
wished him to get in, but he shook his head and declined,
saying that I was to go on to look for a place to camp. I
found out afterwards that he looked upon the breaking of the
pole as a bad omen. I must not forget to mention that I had
bought him some tents, so that, in camping out, he was quite
comfortable, and seemed to enjoy the novelty. This day a
great number of small buck were again killed, but wood being
scarce where we camped, the people had a hard night of it, as
it was very cold and there was very little shelter. The next
morning we started in the same manner, hunting on the way.
In the evening a lot of the men of Upper Zululand, under
Cetywayo's brother, joined us. Cetywayo, in order to show
off, had all his men, who had guns, collected in a body and on
our arrival at the kraal we were going to sleep at that night,
he made them fire two volleys. He had me always close to
him to show the up-country Zulus that he had made me his
friend. On starting from this place—the Umkindwini—he
said that, after the first hunt, he would ride in the carriage,
and that I was to go on and wait for him, as he saw that the
broken pole stood all right. So I went on for about six miles

and waited for him. On reaching me, after a little hesitation, he got in. I think more on account of feeling tired than of any inclination to ride for riding sake. But after we had gone on about a mile or two, he seemed to enjoy it, and was greatly delighted to see some of his big, stout followers who were—an odd collection—our escort on horseback, making ludicrous exertions to keep up with our pace, as I had four good horses in front of me ; so that, as I say, they had to do their utmost to make their poor ponies keep at all near to us. The escort included several dignitaries, such as Sirayo, Gouzi, and several others of the same stamp. They could not possibly have kept up to us if I had not taken compassion on them, in spite of Cetywayo's urging me to push on. I knew from experience that I would only have caused a bad feeling against me for leaving them behind, as some time elapsed before they forgave me for out-pacing them in going to the Mangwini kraal Cetywayo was in high glee when we got to our camping place in the evening, and said he would ride the whole distance in the trap the next day. But the night's rest again made him alter his mind, or perhaps he had again been persuaded not to ride. So that in the morning he walked.

We got to our camping ground on the Imtonjanini early. It was on the exact spot where Cetywayo was re-installed in the year 1883, on his return from England. We expected to meet all the people from the northern parts this day. This evening he was very liberal and gave his followers sixty head of cattle to kill for their suppers. It was the custom of the head Indunas to come to my camp every evening to have something to warm them, as the weather was very cold. On this evening I asked Sirayo what the order of proceedings was to be on our meeting the up-country people. He said, " You ask of us who have come

every evening to ask of you. How should we know what is
to be done ? Have we ever put a King on the throne before ?
You must tell us. Have you not spoken to Cetywayo as to
what is to be done ? "   I said I had not, and as there were so
many rumours about what was to take place, one being that
the Northern Zulus were going to take Cetywayo by force,
we had better go to him in a body and ask him, as, if there
was any fighting to be done, we ought to be prepared, but I
told them I was surprised at their not knowing the order of
procedure, as also at their not consulting Cetywayo about it
My proposal was agreed to, and so we went in a body to the
tent of the latter which was about a hundred yards away.
We found him in very good spirits, and, on my mentioning
the purpose of our errand—as I was spokesman—he seemed
much amused and burst out laughing. He said, "are you
then afraid ?" I said, " No, I am not, but the Indunas here
are, as they don't know what is to take place." He was surprised, however, at what I had told him, and at the Indunas
—much older men than he—being so thoroughly ignorant,
and said, " Is it then true what John Dunn says ? Are you
really not joking ? Why did you not speak to me before ? "
He then went into a lot of details with them, in which I took
not much interest as I began to think seriously of the situation, and began also to be a little suspicious of their (the
Indunas') interest in what was to take place, and that if they
were really anxious about the King, why they had not con-
sulted with him as to what was to be done, as I thought that,
as a matter of course, everything had been settled. I now
recollected that on several occasions, when I had asked any of
them about Uhamu, I had always got an evasive answer, and
as no one seemed to know what Uhamu's intentions were, or
whether he would be with the northern people or not, I began
to feel that there was every likelihood of a fight, and if so,

Cetywayo would not be the favourite of his own party, which they professed he was. After sitting with him till late, I returned to my camp, having learnt what the order of the proceedings was to be, which was, that the whole of the following were to collect in a body, and not to scatter. Accordingly next morning, as soon as it was warm enough, a move was made and all the armed force was collected and formed into a circle, and the order for the advance given. It was a fine sight to see these thousands move off. Cetywayo, with myself, and few followers, took the lead, he still walking. Our course lay over the brow of a hill, on arriving at which he ordered a halt of the followers ; whilst we—the staff—proceeded about half a mile in advance to a knoll, his object being to have a good view of his followers. He then ordered an advance, and so we went on for about three miles and encamped, as this was the spot he had decided to remain at until the whole nation was collected. This spot was the Makeni, not far from the slaughter of the Boers by Dingaan. We were at this spot for about three days until that of the great meeting was at length announced. I had secured a photographer for this occasion, but owing to the cloudy weather and the water being bad, he could not succeed in taking a good picture. I had stationed him at a capital spot, and led Cetywayo, in full dress, and with all his staff, to within fifty yards of where he was. The failure was a great disappointment, and a very great loss to the public in general and to posterity, as such a sight no man will ever again have the opportunity of witnessing, and I believe the photographer, and myself, are the only whitemen who have ever seen a similar sight..

From what I could make of the gathering, there were three distinct bodies, firstly, Cetywayo and his followers ; then came Uhamu and Umnyamana, and a lot of their followers, and then the largest body of all, who were from the north-east, and led by Usibepu. Masipula, although Prime Minister, made his appearance, but with no particular followers. I was very much surprised at there being no one who seeme d to know what was to take place.

CHAPTER VI.

The ground round about where the photographer was stationed was selected for the assembly, and as soon as we— *i.e.*, Cetywayo, myself, and the staff of the former-—arrived on the spot, the north-eastern party moved in sight, and, on getting about half-a-mile from us, they commenced to form in order. From what I could make out from the remarks made around me, I gathered that our people were beginning to feel uneasy, and now believed in the rumour that Cetywayo was to be taken by force. I now thought it time to speak to Cetywayo, which I did, and while I was talking, Sibebu's party made an advance. Uhamu, Umnyamana, and their party were setting on a mound to the west, so that if mischief was meant, we were between two fires, which showed very bad generalship on the part of Cetywayo. Usibepu's party first advanced slowly, and then came on with a rush, and some of Cetywayo's staff—Undconewane, who subsequently was with him when he was presented to the Queen in London, amongst others—began to prepare for flight. I alone told Cetywayo that unless the advancing party was stopped, there would be a fight. I had nothing in my hand, by the way, but my hunting-crop. From the expression on Cetywayo's face when he answered me, I could see that he had never considered the danger. " Imbala," said he (meaning, " You don't say so ?") I said, " Yes, don't you see ? Send some

Incekus at once to stop them," which he immediately did.
On looking round to the hill on the west of us, I could see
that the party with Uhamu and Umnyamana had also taken
the alarm. I could now see that Cetywayo began to take a
more serious view of the situation. He gave quiet orders for
our party to arm themselves, as we had come on to the ground
unarmed—at least Cetywayo's followers had, but I had 200
of my hunters with me. These were always in the habit of
carrying their guns and ammunition with them, so that I,
with them, could make a stand. Fortunately, on the arrival
of Cetywayo's messengers, the leaders of Usibepu's party had
influence enough to stop the advance, or else there certainly
would have been great slaughter. This fact I found out long
afterwards. As soon as I saw the check in Usibepu's party,
I left Cetywayo, who I could see did not know exactly how
to act, and passing through my men to give them confidence
—telling them, however, to prepare for the worst—and after
telling one of my men who I knew to be a bad shot, that, in the
event of a scrimmage, I would take his gun, I walked quietly
up to where Umnyamana was sittting. As soon as he saw me
he got up and came towards me, calling out to Uhamu to
come also. As soon as he reached me he took hold of my
hand, and said, "What is this you are doing? Why are
you arming your party?" This I laughed at, saying, "Why
should we arm? Who have we to fear?" He said, "All
right; remain with us, then"; to which I assented. I had
left Cetywayo without telling him where I was going. Shortly
after I had been with Umnyamana, I saw Cetywayo's party
coming up to where we were. Whether he had missed me,
and not knowing where I was had got uneasy, or whether he
had changed his mind as to the place of assembly, I can't say,
but he came up to where I was, and the whole of the parties
then came up and formed a great circle. As each lot came

up it fired blank charges, but they fired so close to one another
in some instances that there was a serious danger of being
knocked over by the powder. In fact, Sedcweledcwele, one
of the principal men on our side, and Colonel of the Ngobamakosi Regiment, had a charge so closely fired behind him
that the paper and wadding from the gun cut a hole in his
cows tails, which comprised a principal part of his dress, and
also burnt a hole in his shoulder. If the man who had fired
the shot had had his gun loaded with a heavy charge of
powder the affair-might have proved fatal. Everything, however, passed off quietly, and I firmly believe that it was owing
to my advising Cetywayo to send messengers to check
Usibepu's party in their advance that a general massacre was
avoided. Another check on the opposite party was the knowledge of the fact that my hunters were there with their deadly
guns, and the opposite chiefs also knew that those of Cetywayo's
men who were armed with guns, and considered to be under
me, were also present. The whole ceremony seemed to be a
novelty to all, old as well as young, as they had no precedent
to go by. After all was over Cetywayo sent for me and we
returned to his private tent (a photograph of which was
taken) and after a talk on various matters, and a drink of
Kafir beer, which I much enjoyed, I returned to my camp.
This night the whole of the nation were assembled. That is
to say, the male part, but as a matter of fact a good portion
of the girls and young married women were also present, I
felt very much disappointed again at the photographer not
having been able to take a good picture. The next day
another meeting took place, but the number of the people had
greatly diminished. On this day Cetywayo was proclaimed
King by Masipula, the Prime Minister, and, so far, the ceremony ended for a time. All this time we were awaiting the
arrival of Mr. Shepstone, and after the lapse of three days

without any news of him, the King decided to move on to
the vicinity of Nodwengo Kraal. On arriving close there
he, owing to some superstition, struck off from the main road,
across country, not going near the Nodwengo Kraal. His
object in thus doing was to keep the site of the intended kraal
a secret in order that the abatagati (according to Native
superstition) or wizards might not bewitch the spot.

Nothing of any particular interest took place for several
days. At last it was announced that Somseu had crossed the
Tugela on his way up, and eventually reported as being at
the Intonjanini, from where he sent a messenger to say he
expected to have found the King awaiting him there, and
that, as he had not done so, he hoped to see Cetywayo there
as soon as convenient. But the latter strongly objected to
this course, as did most of his headmen. The King then
asked me to go to Mr. Shepstone with some of his messengers, but I objected, as I did not wish to be involved in the
dispute. I said, at the same time, that I thought he (the
King) was quite right, but advised him to send some men of
standing instead of the usual class of messengers. He sent
Sibepu and Sirayo to settle matters, and it was a day or two
after their return that a party of Mr. Shepstone's escort rode
over. Amongst them were Lewis Reynolds, and the late Mr.
Baines, the traveller, and two officers, one of whom was Major
Clark, of Transvaal notoriety, their object being to see if
everything was on the square, as they expressed it. On my
stating my views, they quite agreed with me, that there was
no danger, and they themselves were anxious to come on. I
must not forget to mention an amusing incident connected
with this party. No sooner were they seated in my tent
than old Baines asked for a piece of paper, and he at once
commenced to make a sketch with his pencil, which, on finishing, he handed to us, saying, " I defy any of you to sketch

yourself in the act of falling from a horse." It appeared that
that morning whilst *en route* to me, they had galloped across
country, and Baines' horse had put his foot in a hole and
fallen with him. It was a very good natural sketch. They
returned to their camp the same day well pleased with their
ride, and fully determined to persuade Mr. Shepstone to come
on to a spot near to where I was with the King. Whilst
waiting to receive Somseu, the King decided to have a hunt,
and to sleep out. We did not, however, go far the first afternoon, as it was late before a start was made, and only a few
small buck were killed. We encamped for the night in the
Bush. The next morning an early start was made, and the
people thrown out to surround a tract of country about four
miles in diameter, and by twelve o'clock a lot of game of all
sorts were killed. I only managed to get a shot at one buck,
which I killed, as there was difficulty in free firing owing to
the people about ; indeed, it was wonderful that no accident
happened for the bullets were flying about in every direction.
About one o'clock the King gave the order to return home.
It was a very hot day, and as he had had nothing to eat since
supper, I expect he began to feel the want of something. I
myself had taken the precaution to put a couple of biscuits
in my pocket. As I said before, it was a very hot day, and I
expected to see the King perspiring profusely ; but, on the
contrary, to my surprise he kept as dry as a bone. This
shows what hard condition he must have been in. To all
appearance he was fat, but on touching his flesh it became
apparent that it was all firm flesh. This is a peculiarity of all
his family. They have all immense thighs. There are only
two of his relations, to my knowledge, who are given to be
flabby, viz., Uhamu and Mahanana. This peculiarity
points to the fact that they are a distinct tribe, and it is a
great pity that no history has been traced. This, as I have

said, I attempted to do, but was frustrated by the loss of all
my notes, notes which no man will ever again have the opportunity of taking.

CHAPTER VII.

Cetywayo's ancestors descended from the younger son,
Zulu ; his elder brother being Quabe, the founder of the
present races known by that title, the representatives of whom
are the present Musi and Mafongonyana, now living in Natal.
The quarrel between Quabe and Zulu, the two brothers,
occurred about a white cow, bought by their mother, and
given by her to Zulu. This much enraged Quabe, and hence
the strife and the breaking up of the family. Pongosi, the
ancestor of the present tribe of that name, of whom the late
Gauzi (one of the Chiefs appointed by Sir Garnet, now Lord
Wolseley) was head Induna, and he sided with Zulu, and
collected all his tribe together.

But, to return to our hunt story. On our way back,
a hare jumped up, at which several shots were fired. Cetywayo also fired, and made a good shot, and bowled him over
at about sixty yards. This was not bad, considering that it
was a bullet he fired with. He was in high glee, and said I
could not now laugh at him. But soon after that, I had an
opportunity of distinguishing myself, as I fired when the
whole of the men of the hunt were looking on. As we were
walking along there was suddenly heard a shout of " Inya-
mazana ! " (game) and two Rhee Bucks came cantering over
the brow of a hill about 200 yards off. I called to the King
to shoot, but he would not do so, saying they were too far. I
then took sight and made a good shot, hitting one in the
head and so, of course, rolled him over. Cetywayo shouted

out some expression of praise, when the whole lot took up the
shout. From this day my reputation as a good shot was
established amongst the nation. The King said to me " I
have often heard of your shooting, but now I am satisfied."
At this moment two men came running towards us, and, on
reaching us, reported that the kraal was on fire. The King
immediately ordered all the men to run as hard as they could
and extinguish the flames, and we followed at a good pace,
broiling hot as it was, and still he did not perspire. Sure
enough, as soon as we got in sight, we saw the King's kraal
was in a blaze, but, before we got up to it, the fire had been
put out, but not before it had demolished a great portion of
the huts, and scorched a good many people ; one man and a girl
in particular were badly burnt. Although the fire at the
kraal had been extinguished, it had passed on, and was still
raging in the grass (which was very dry) away to the West.
The King's huts and tents had fortunately escaped, so on
getting to these, we went in, and he called for some beer, but
before taking any he took a drink of water. I never saw
such a change come over a man. About ten seconds after he
had drunk the water he broke out into profuse perspiration,
which simply streamed from him at every pore. This lasted
for about a quarter-of-an-hour, when he began to get dry.

After finishing the beer I went to my camp, which I had
just reached when there was a cry of fire again, and on going
out I saw that the wind had changed, and the fire was raging
along, making for the kraal, which it soon reached, burning
down the huts, and a few minutes after came charging for
my camp, where stood a wagon of mine with a lot of ammunition. I at once set all the hands I could muster on to it, and
ran it into an old bare mealie garden, not however, before the
fire had overtaken it, and scorched some of the fellows' legs,
but they bravely stuck to it and saved it. In the meantime I

had collected all the men I could to carry water in calabashes to me. These I emptied all round the enclosure where my tents were standing, which checked the flames and gave us time to beat them out, not, however, before some of the fence had caught fire within two yards of my sleeping tent. I can assure you, reader, I breathed with a sense of relief when the furious flames passed on beyond my camp without doing any serious damage. In the adjacent kraal—one of Cetywayo's—more than half of the huts were consumed, his own again escaping. Many of the poor people had a hard night of it, as no shelter was to be had, and all their blankets were destroyed, as the fire came on so suddenly that they had no time to save anything, and there was a good deal of grumbling and ironical good wishes for Mr. Shepstone for detaining them so long.

At last the Natal Representative was reported as approaching, and he shortly after took up his position about three miles from us. All this time the people were under the impression that Umbulazi was being brought up by Mr. Shepstone, and all his actions were therefore looked upon with suspicion, and closely watched. A day of meeting was at length fixed on. The King first intended to go with me in the carriage, but he was persuaded by his headmen from doing so, as they were afraid that, if any treachery was brewing, I might drive off with him at a gallop and hand him over to the English, so he asked me to go on with the carriage and await him. He shortly afterwards followed, with about fifty of his principal men. Whilst I was talking with Mr. Shepstone they came in sight, but walking very slowly, the pace getting slower as they got nearer. I could see the King expected someone to come and meet him, so I asked Mr. Shepstone to allow me to do so. He answered that he would be glad if I would do so, and thus give Cetywayo confidence, also saying that when the King came within a hundred yards, he would also step out to meet him. This was accordingly carried out, and after a short talk, Mr. Shepstone, with Cetywayo and some of his followers, retired to a tent to consult on different subjects. Whilst this was going on inside, an amusing scene was taking place outside between two Iszibongi (jesters or praisers), each yelling out the strings of praises of their respective Chiefs—Mr. Shepstone and Cetywayo—and trying to outdo each other. At last they got so excited, being urged on by the crowd of whites and blacks who had formed a ring round them, that they were very nearly coming to blows. Seeing the matter was getting serious I stepped in and separated them by taking Cetywayo's man away. The scene had indeed been highly diverting. The lively and extraordinary grimaces and the other visual contortions of the men must have been very edifying to anyone who had never witnessed such a scene before. After a day had been fixed for another preliminary meeting to consult, the King and I drove to my camp.

The second meeting took place at the Umlambongwenya Kraal, at which the King was staying for a time. This assembly took place in the middle of the cattle kraal, and was attended only by Mr. Shepstone and one of his sons, and the late Colonel Durnford, and also by three or four of Mr. Shepstone's Native Indunas, on the one side, and of Cetywayo, myself, and a few of his men on the other. Nothing of importance transpired, and after a talk which lasted some time, I opened a couple of bottles of champagne and claret—a favourite blended drink of mine—and mixed them in a tin can, when several of us refreshed ourselves, Cetywayo included.

At this meeting the subject of Amatonga labour was brought up, and Mr. Shepstone proposed that an agent be

appointed by Government. The King agreed to the introduction of the labourers, but, turning to me, he said, " There
is no need to appoint anyone ; here is one that will do."
Mr. Shepstone remarked to me that he did not know if I
would accept the position. I said that I would if I was well
paid for it.

CHAPTER VIII.

Before proceeding further, I must retrace my steps and
finish the story about the fire. The evening after the day of
the great fire, I was sent for by the Indunas who wished to consult me on some matters, and whilst sitting with them in the
hut, a cry of fire was again raised. The grass was so dry
that before anything could be done twenty or thirty huts were
burned down so close to Cetywayo's quarters that the people
of his household huddled all the things out and carried them
some distance. A good deal of pilfering went on, and many
of the things were never seen again. Amongst the things
was a tin box containing about two dozen bottles of Chlorodyne that I had bought for him. · This pilfering showed what
little fear these people have for death, well knowing that on
the slightest thing being found in their possession, and which
belonged to the King, death followed for a certainty. Cetywayo was very down-hearted on account of these fires, and
said openly that he did not think they were the result of
accident, but were lit intentionally, and he began to be very
suspicious.

The day was now finally fixed for the great ceremony of
the Coronation of Cetywayo by Mr. Shepstone, with which,
however, the former was not at all satisfied. What he had
expected he never revealed, but expressed himself as being
disappointed with what took place, which was nothing but a

D

lecture of advice. There was a very small show of people, most of them being tired of waiting so long, and having returned to their homes. The photographer again failed to take a picture although I had secured him a good position within the kraal. This was again a disappointment as it ought to have been a good picture. There had been a large Marquee erected, which, with a lot or things, were made a present to Cetywayo after the ceremony was over. After Mr. Shepstone and all the escort had left, the King went into the Marquee to inspect the things. Here he was again disappointed as there was not a single thing he could put to his own use. And so all the ceremony was over. He had been proclaimed King by Masipula before the arrival of Mr. Shepstone, and now this had merely been confirmed by him, and now he was the acknowledged King of the country by the Natal Government, as well as by the Zulus.

The next day Mr. Shepstone broke up his camp and set off for Natal, and so we were once more left to ourselves to do as we liked, a proof of which was shown a few days afterwards. As the last of the staff of Sir Theophilus (as he is now known—having received this title in 1876) was moving off, I was sitting with the King in his hut, when two messengers from Sir Theophilus were announced. They stated that they had orders to deliver their message personally to the King, and he gave orders for them to be brought in—at the same time saying to me " Sit on one side so that the messengers cannot see you." On their arrival he told them to sit outside the hut and deliver their message, which was simply relating to me. They said they had been sent by Sir Theophilus, and that though he had assented to my being appointed Amatonga Agent, the King must not deem this to be conclusive, as the Governor of Natal might object to me and appoint someone else. On the King asking if that was all, they assented. He then said, Tell Somseu that that question is settled, I want no one else."

Soon after the above, Sir Theophilus wrote me a rather severe letter, I thought, warning me not to assume too much authority, as he could not recognise it. At this I felt much hurt, as I had given no cause for his saying so, and in answer, wrote him to that effect, and to my letter I received the following answer :—

Pietermaritzburg, September 29th 1873.

DEAR SIR,—

You seem to have entirely misunderstood the object of my note of the 4th from Emtonjanini. My intention was to assist, not to find fault with you. Of course I perfectly understood what you meant by speaking of your protector to the bearers, but I know at the same time, that others would not, and if I had not put that right, I should have been accused of having set you up as an independent power in Zululand, or having acknowledged you as possessing such independent power. It was to avoid an inference which I am sure you never intended that I wrote what I did. I had no notion that you interfered with my proposal to Cetywayo on the labour question, and never intended to hint at such a thing— on the contrary, I am satisfied that if you undertake the matter, your personal ability and your position too will enable you to do it a great deal better than anyone else—so please discharge from your mind any idea you may have entertained that I wished or intended to find fault with you. What I meant by being more precise is this. Your proposal has to be submitted to the Legislative Council, and it is a matter that interests everyone, and upon which everyone will wish to know every particular—for instance, your own salary of £250, and £30 a year for horse hire is plain enough, that means £280 a year—then you say, pay for six men—but you do not

D2

say at what rate.   So that remains an open point—it may be
10s. or 15s. for Zulus, or £5 a month for white men.   This
wants your explanation to enable me to support your proposal.
Then again you say your stations for food and shelter would
be at a distance of forty or fifty miles over a length of 150,
and that the food of each labourer should be mealies, mealie
meal, or sweet potatoes, for which 6d. a feed is to be paid.
The planters and the Council will want to know what they
are paying their 6d. for.   Why not say that there will be
four or five stations, as you think necessary, and that for
each feed to *consist of so much mealies, mealie meal, or sweet
potatoes* 6d. will have to be paid?   We should all then know
that five stations at 6d. each feed would mean 2s. 6d. for so
much food spent over a certain distance.

Please understand distinctly that, in writing this way, my
object is to help you to succeed, not to find fault.   I am much
interested in your success as you are or can be, and I wish to
avoid every point upon which I see it possible that fault may
be found with your proposal.   I was quite satisfied with the
manner in which Cetywayo behaved in the matter, but I was
afraid he did not see the deep importance of it to the people
of Natal ; indeed it was quite impossible that he should, and
I endeavoured to impress it upon him by frequent reference.
In all his dealings with me I found him remarkably straight-
forward and intelligent, and am very much pleased that the
Zulus have got a man to reign over them who is so far in
advance of them in sagacity and foresight.   I hope you will
fully understand the spirit this letter is written in.   I support
your project by asking you to give me all the necessary
information to do so.

Yours, truly,

(Signed)   T. SHEPSTONE.

P.S.—" The Council meeting has been put off in consequence of the illness of the Governor, so you will have plenty
of time to give me all the particulars I want."

However I got the appointment of Amatonga Agent at a salary of £300 a year, and retained it until the war broke out. I encountered a deal of difficulty for some time, as it had been the custom of the Zulu people to look upon the Amatongas as objects of legitimate plunder ; but having been fully authorised by Cetywayo to do as I thought fit, I soon set matters right, and they still continue unmolested to this day.

One afternoon it was reported by one of the King's Incekus, or household servants, that a tin can resembling the one that had disappeared on the night of the fire, with the chlorodyne in it, was at the kraal of another Inceku, who had gone home the day after the fire, and who was residing on the coast. The King at once sent off a man to see. This man pretended to be on a visit to the suspected man, and whilst at the kraal of the latter the tin was produced by the thief, saying he was going to give his visitor a treat of some grog he had bought, and which was very nice. On this he took out about half-a-dozen bottles of chlorodyne and emptied them into a pot of beer, which he gave to his wives. The stuff, being sweet, would naturally give a good flavour to the beer, which the ladies soon finished. The description that I got from the witness of the scene that follows was very amusing, as these people are very happy in their manner of relating anecdotes, &c. Shortly after the women had finished the beer, they began to yawn and laugh consumedly at each other, each accusing the other of making her yawn. This went on for some little time, much to the amusement of the spectators and the husband, who himself was getting nearly as bad, owing to having taken a couple of mouthfuls of the drug himself. At last they could not keep their eyes open, and they were eventually taken out of the hut insensible, and their state was put down to the strength of the supposed spirits. The women were, of course, very ill for some days afterwards, and one was nearly dying. As soon as the man who had been sent by the King, saw the effects of the chlorodyne, he quietly sent off to inform the latter, and in about two days a messenger came to summon him, as well as the man who had stolen the can. One morning, about eight o'clock, I was sitting in front of one of my wagons talking to some of my men when I saw a gathering of the Indunas at the gate of the King's kraal. I remarked that there was some mischief brewing. After they had been talking for some little while, I saw all at once a scrimmage, and a man knocked down and pounced on. Seeing me in view, the Indunas sent to tell me that they had been trying the thief, and that he was to be killed. The poor fellow lay on the ground for a short time, for he had only been stunned. His arms had been twisted right round behind his head and tied together straight over his head. As soon as he recovered his senses he prepared to march. Having often witnessed a similar scene he knew, from terrible experience, the routine. So he got up of his own accord, and without being told, took the path to the place of execution, and was followed by about half-a-dozen men, who had been told off to go and finish him.

This was the first man killed after the coronation of Cetywayo, almost before Sir Theo. Shepstone could have reached Maritzburg. But it served the fellow right, as he was guilty of a great breach of trust. The Zulu is only to be ruled by fear of death, or the confiscation of his entire property.

The policy at present adopted by the Home Government is only making the fine Zulu nation a race of rogues, who will eventually stick at nothing. The alteration in them during the last five years is something astonishing. The most noticeable but unaccountable thing is the spirit of in-

vention—to put it mildly—that seems to have sprung up
suddenly amongst them. At one time almost anything told
was to be believed, but, in these days, one has to be very
cautious in believing anything, as many of them will invent
and twist, and turn a tale to suit their own views, without
the slightest regard to truth.

I must not omit to mention an event of great note which
took place about the time of the Coronation. This was the
death of Masipula, the Prime Minister. He had been to a
meeting of the principal Indunas held at a temporary kraal
or encampment where Cetywayo was residing until he took
up his position as king. The meeting was rather a strong
one, I was told, as I was not at it, having received a hint that
my presence was not necessary, as the subject of discussion
was only the rule of the late King Umpande. On the breaking up of the meeting Masipula called on me as he was passing to his kraal where he resided. After sitting with me for
some time in my tent, he got up to leave, and turning to me,
said, " Good-bye, child of Mr. Dunn, I have finished my part
and am now going to lie down—*I am now going to sleep*—look
after your own affairs—I have no more a voice in matters "
—meaning that he wished to retire from public life, as
Umpande, to whom he had been chief Induna, was dead, and
so he now wished to end his days in peace. The poor old
fellow little thought, when he thus spoke, that his end was so
near—that the words he then said to me were among his last
and that the sleep he wished for was to be everlasting, for
that same evening, as soon as he got to the Umlambongwenya
kraal, where he was staying, on entering his hut, he was
suddenly taken ill, and died before morning. There was, of
course, much consternation amongst the people, and, as usual,
many rumours afloat, one of which was, that having displeased
the King, something had been put into his beer.

Shortly after the killing of the Chlorodyne man, one of
Pande's old servants was put to death and this was the
opening of the ball of killing without trial which was usual
in Cetywayo's reign.

CHAPTER IX.

About a month after his coronation, Cetywayo gave
orders for all of the late King's cattle to be collected and
brought to him. In due course of time the cattle were reported to be in the vicinity, and he appointed a day for the
first lot to be brought. It was a wonderful sight to behold
the continuous stream of cattle, from day to day for more
than a week. As soon as one lot passed, another came, according with the different military kraals the system of the
apportioning of these cattle also according with the numbers
taken in battle which, as above stated, were distributed
amongst the military kraals. The cattle were now again distributed by the Indunas to men who became responsible to
them, and reported to them all deaths of cattle, and they in
their turn again reported to the King. Consequently, rightly
speaking, these cattle were the property of the State, the
same as the land was, and were supposed to be drawn upon
for state purposes, even although considered to be the property of the King. But he himself would not take any
number from any particular kraal, without first consulting the
Indunas in charge of such cattle, even if he wanted any for
slaughter. In the same way he would not part with any of
the land of the country without first consulting the leading
men, and only, with their consent, could he do so. I will
quote an instance. Some years ago, the Natal Land and
Colonization Company made a proposal to me to try and
secure for them the title of a certain tract of land in the Zulu

Country. Accordingly I spoke to Cetywayo on the subject although he was not King then. He seemed well pleased with the tempting offer I made him, and appointed a meeting with me, as also with some of the Company, to meet him and his head men. Accordingly I went to D'Urban and the Company selected a man to return with me. On getting near the Tulwana kraal, I went on to announce my arrival, and a meeting was appointed for next day. On our arrival at the kraal we found a large gathering of the headmen seated with Cetywayo. After the usual greeting, Cetywayo said to me "Speak." I then spoke on the subject in hand. After several of the Indunas had asked a few questions, Umnyama spoke and said, "Yes, what you say, child of Mr. Dunn, is very good, but our land is our home, we don't like parting with it ; besides, we are afraid of you white men. If we give you a piece for more than one to live on, they will want more, and so on, until they get the whole, and we will have to wander about as if we had no land. It is well with you personally. You are living with us—you are one of us, but we don't know any other whiteman." Cetywayo turned to me, and said, "You hear ? I can say no more—the Indunas have conquered me." Thus ended our land scheme, all this proving that the King was ruled by the voice of the Indunas in matters of cattle and land. Cetywayo though not King at the time, yet had all the power of a King.

The cattle came pouring in day after day. Out of each lot the King selected some fancy coloured, and gave many cattle away as presents. He obliged me to be with him the whole of the time, and I got heartily sick of sitting with him and looking on. I estimated the number of cattle at about one hundred thousand head. After all was over he made me a present of one hundred head of young stock, and the whole lot were again dispersed. But this particular

muster ended in serious disaster. It was the death-blow to
cattle breeding in Zululand. "Lungsickness" had been,
and was very busy with many of the herds collected, and
mixing them up spread the disease all over the country, and
judging from the number of hides that the traders carried
from the country during the two following years, the number
of cattle must have been reduced by at least a half. So that
Zululand, from being one of the richest, is now one of the
poorest cattle countries in this part of South Africa, and I
believe it will never be one-half as well off in cattle as in the
olden day. Oxen are at present very scarce, and the Zulus
set a greater value on an ox than a whiteman does. After
having been with the King four months from the time of my
starting from the Ondine, he gave his consent to my returning
home, and right glad was I to do so.

Things after this went on well and peacefully, owing, I
am sure, to nothing but my having advised Cetywayo, and
shown—to the intimidation of the rival factions—that he
could produce a good stand of arms. Otherwise I am convinced that there would have been bloodshed at the first
meeting of all the Zulu tribes before the arrival of Sir Theo.,
who established him as King, so that he owed his position to
the countenance of the English, when he was not a favourite
with the Natives.

All now remained quiet until he took it into his head
that he ought to establish his supremacy by following out an
ancient custom of washing the spears of the nation in the
blood of some neighbouring tribe. When he conceived this
idea, he sent for me to write a letter to the Natal Government, stating his wish to go against the Amaswazi. To this
he received the following reply, on the margin of the despatch
(now in my possession) containing the reply, the autograph
of Sir Benj. Chilley Campbell Pine, is affixed :—

Reply of His Excellency Sir Benjamin Chilley Campbell Pine, K.C.M.G., Lieut.-Governor of Natal, to Cetywayo, Chief of the Zulu Nation.

Office of Secretary for Native Affairs,

October 22, 1874.

"The Lieutenant-Governor has received the letter sent by Cetywayo, and the reasons given for making war upon the Amaswazi.

"The Lieutenant-Governor sees no cause whatever for making war, and informs Cetywayo that such an intention on the part of the Zulus meets with his entire disapproval.

"Cetywayo must also remember that the Amaswazi are almost entirely surrounded by white people who have settled in the country, and it will be impossible for the Zulus, if war is made, to avoid geting into difficulties with them.

"Many years ago the Lieutenant-Governor sent a letter to the late King M'Pande, requesting him to allow the Amaswazi to live in peace from any further attacks from the Zulus, he promised to do so, and kept his word.

"The Lieutenant-Governor trusts that what he has said will be sufficient to deter Cetywayo and the Zulu Nation from entertaining such a project.

"By command of His Excellency,

"(Signed)   J. W. SHEPSTONE,

"Acting Secretary for Native Affairs."

The above letter made the King change his plans, although it enraged him, as I could plainly see. A journey of eighty miles which I had frequently to make to the King's place was no joke for me, but there was no help for it ; and, as my argument had weight with him, whenever he had a difficult question to unravel, the Indunas always advised him

to send for me, consequently I had constantly to be going
backwards and forwards. On one of these occasions he sent
for me to read a letter purporting to have come from the
Government in Pietermaritzburg. On his handing the supposed despatch to me, I was surprised to find it to be an appointment of a Dr. Smith and a Mr. Colenso to act for him
(the King) as his agents in all diplomatic affairs connected
with the Colonial Government. On my saying to him,
" This is no message—where is the other letter ?"—thinking
there was some mistake, he said that it was the only one. I
then told him the purport of the document, at the same time
asking him who these men were that he had appointed. His
answer was, " I am the same as you ; I don't know them—or
anything written on that paper ; the words are not mine."
He then sent for the messengers (his own, who had returned
to him), and on their arrival, he asked them the meaning of
what was in the letter they had brought. Their answer was,
" Yes, we delivered the King's message as it was given to us,
but on going to Sobantu (the late Bishop Colenso)
he advised us to make the statement we did, and as we
thought it was for the good of our King, we did so—Sobantu
further stating that if the King trusted to the Inhlwana of
Sonzica (meaning the Little House of the Shepstone's) he
would go astray, as they (the Shepstone's) had to leave the
Amaxoza country for having got them (the Amaxoza) into
trouble with the whites, and they would treat Cetywayo likewise unless he appointed some white men to look after his
interests with the Government of Natal, proposing the before
named gentlemen to be such agents." I advised Cetywayo
at once to rectify the mistake, which he agreed to, and sent
off messengers to the Government. Not long after the return
of the messengers from Natal, Mr. Colenso came into Zululand to get an explanation from Cetywayo, and to claim

certain expenses which he thought himself entitled to in consequence of the appointment. On arriving at the Amahlabatine he took up his quarters with Mr. Mullins, a trader, and one morning he came over to my camp and explained his mission to me, requesting me to assist in his recovering from Cetywayo the sum of five hundred pounds, a sum he said he felt he was entitled to. I, knowing the circumstances, tried to persuade him that he was wrong, and that there was small probability of his getting redress, at the same time declining to intercede for him. At a meeting between himself and Cetywayo I was present, and after going into particulars, Cetywayo spoke out very straightforwardly, saying that although he looked upon Sobantu (Bishop Colenso) as a friend and a father, he did not wish him or his to interfere between him and the Government.

Not long after this the King confided to me that he had been told not to put his trust in me, as I had been offered a box full of money, and all the land along the coast, if I would kill him, at the same time saying " I tell you because I don't believe this, but I wont tell you who says this. It is, however, one of your own race. I think this is said against you from jealousy." I tried hard to get him to reveal who had been trying to make this mischief between him and me, but he would not divulge the secret.

CHAPTER X.

About this time a fight took place between two sections of the Undini kraal, the Tulwana and Ugobamakosi, two separate regiments, but located in the same kraal. This was at the Umkosi, or Meeting of the Feast of First Fruits. I was sitting with the King in the Nodwengo kraal, where he

was holding state, and several regiments had been going
through the prescribed ceremonies, when, on looking towards
the Ulundi kraal, (which was about a mile and a half away)
to see if the regiments mentioned were coming out, I saw
that some scrimmage was going on, and said so to Cetywayo,
but he asked "Between who? they all belong to the same
kraal." But I still persisted and said that although it was so,
yet there was something wrong. Just at that moment we
could distinctly see that one body was charging another right
through my camp which was opposite the Ulundi kraal. The
King then said I was right, and sent off some men to see what
was wrong. They were not away long before they returned
stating that there was a severe fight between the Tulwana and
Ngobamakosi regiments, and that they (the messengers)
could only approach within a certain distance for fear of being
killed, as the latter regiment gave no quarter to a man with a
ring on. (For the information of such of my readers as may
not be acquainted with the peculiarities of this people, I may
say that at a certain mature age the men are allowed to
encircle their heads with a ring which is worked on to a rim
of hair left on the clean shaved head, and composed of cow-
dung, ungiane—a sticky exudation from the Mimosa and other
trees—grease, &c.) Fresh messengers were sent by the King
to stop the fighting, but without effect, and so it went on
until nightfall, and as I saw no chance of the fight abating
I went back to my camp, telling my men to keep close to me,
knowing that they would not be molested so long as it was
known that they were in my personal charge. On our way,
several parties of the Ngobamakosi, who were lying in ambush
to cut off any of the Tulwana who might be returning, sprung
up and ran close up to my party with assegai drawn, but as
soon as I called out, saying it was me, they drew back.

On getting back to my camp I found a sanguinary mess. On lighting up in my tent I found that one poor fellow must have run for refuge there and been stabbed in the tent, as there was a squirt of blood right round the canvass, over the table, and covering a Worcester Sauce bottle and salt cellar all over. On going to my sleeping tent I also found the front of it all covered with blood, and my servants told me that one man had been killed there, whom they had dragged outside, and there he lay about three yards from my wagon. Another was lying against the fence where my cook had his kitchen. This poor fellow was not dead, but unconscious, and moaning frightfully. I tried to get him to drink some water, and then tried to make him swallow some spirits, but he was too far gone and died during the course of the night. All round the cattle kraal the dead and wounded were lying, and everything was covered with blood, the hottest of the fight having taken place there. Feeling rather hungry after the long day, and having performed my ablutions, I went to my dining tent expecting to find the table laid as usual, but was surprised to find no preparations. On my calling to my cook and asking for an explanation, the fellow stared at me and said, " where am I to put your food." I told him where it was always put. " What," said he, " With all this blood " ? and he pointed to the tent and table. But I told him to get some water and wash the table, a job he did not at all like, for although Zulus do not mind shedding blood, and ripping a man up in battle, they have, in their cooler moments, a great dread of touching a dead body, or the blood of men. After I had finished dinner and the servant had cleared the table, he said, on leaving the tent " You whitemen are monstrous, you eat your food where blood has been spilt, as if it was water." I gave him a good night-cap and told him not to mind, as neither he nor I would be the worse for it. I

turned in after taking a walk round, and doing what I could
for all the poor fellows who were lying near wounded, but
could not get much sleep owing to the groans of the wounded,
swelled by the cries of friends and relatives calling out to find
some missing one the whole night long. Early the next
morning Dr. Oftebro, and the Rev. Mr. Gundersen, Nor-
wegian Missionaries, came to my camp, and we took a walk
round to see if we could do any good in relieving the
wounded. The doctor had a lot of bandages, &c. Many a
mournful family, sitting in groups, did we meet with, and
sympathetically heard them moaning over some dead or
badly wounded relative. Others again were carrying some
of the dead to be buried. One poor old man we saw, with
his two daughters, sitting over the corpse of his only son.
He seemed quite stupefied with grief, and sadly said to me
" He was my only one." We met with several pools of blood
from where the victims had either got up and gone away, or
had been carried off by their relatives. One poor girl had
only just arrived the same day, having brought food from
home for her two brothers, but since the fight she had heard
nothing of them. She went in search of them and found
them lying side by side, both killed, which so much affected
her that she gave one heart-rending, piercing shriek, and
dropped down dead by their side.

We estimated the killed on both sides to amount to between sixty and seventy. To give an example of the absurd
difference of opinion between some people as to the number of
killed, I was riding with the present Lord Wolseley, after the
battle, over the field of Ulundi, which was near where the fight
above described took place, and talking about the probable number of killed, when I heard a man say to the then Sir Garnet,
that there were more killed in the fight between the two Zulu
regiments than by the troops at Ulundi, and on Sir Garnet

asking him what number, he said he thought between seven and eight hundred. I have said that my estimate was between sixty and seventy.

A great many of the wounded were carried to Mr. Gundersen's Mission Station, and were taken care of by Dr. Oftebro, and he must have had a very trying time of it. With kind attention he brought many round, but some died. I also took charge of several of the wounded who made the fence of my cattle kraal their home for a time, and I did my best for them. A great many of them were buried about two hundred yards from my camp, in gullies and ant bear holes, and the neighbourhood being infested with wolves, they made a hideous howling and great noise over some unfortunates, whilst strange to say, others were untouched. This particularly struck me one morning when I went to the scene of the conflict. One body lay apparently quite exposed, but whilst the wolves had not touched, it, on the other hand, they had disinterred a man who had been very securely buried, having a heap of stones over his grave.

The scent getting rather high around my camp, I was glad of an excuse for returning home, but before doing so I was fortunate enough to be the means of saving the life of Usidcweledcwele, Colonel, or Commander of the Ngobama-kosi Regiment. After this I went over to the Indabakaombi Kraal, where the King was staying, as he—deterred by superstition from passing over the ground where so many had been killed—could not come to me. On my entering his hut he said " Have you heard what happened last night? The Baboon was here again, and left evidences of its presence in the enclosure." This referred to a belief that Usidcwele-dcwele made use of a Baboon which he had power over, to send around his charms of witchcraft, and that he had con-

E

stantly sent this animal at night to lay his charms at the door
of the King's hut, in order that he might be continually in
favour. So if any dog got into the enclosure about the huts
of the King, and left its traces, the matter was laid to the
charge of the said Baboon ; a rather knowing excuse for the
gate keepers to get out of a scrape, and out of clearing up
any impurity, as such dirty work was the duty of certain
medicine doctors. Well, to continue with Cetywayo's account, he said to me, " He does not do this to injure me, but
to turn my heart so that I may not get angry with him. Usidcweledcwele has sent his isilwana (wild beast) as he was
afraid I might kill him after what took place the other day,"
meaning the fight between the regiment of the Colonel in
question and the Tulwana. After a long talk with him, in
which I tried to persuade him not to listen to what was said
against the slandered Colonel, as I knew he was one of his
staunchest adherents, and that what was said against him
was only from jealousy, I went out and whilst walking amongst
the different groups of headmen, I heard a conversation between three of the Indunas, who were sitting apart, which
was to the effect that a message was to be sent to the Colonel
to say that the King wished him to return, and nothing further
would be thought of the fight, and that as soon as the messenger returned and reported that he was on the way, men
were to be sent to way-lay and kill him. To explain the
cause of ill-feeling on this occasion, I must go back to the
fight ; which was supposed to have been caused by the Colonel's assumption of authority in ordering his regiment to
break through the Tulwana one, of which Uhamu was supposed to be in command. After the affair Uhamu went
straight home in high displeasure, and on being sent for, refused to return until Colonel Usidcweledcwele had been
brought to task, and as the King had refused to have him

killed, this tale of the Baboon had been trumped up in hopes of inducing Cetywayo to comply with their wishes. There was also a deadly hatred against the Colonel, on account of his being so great a favourite with the King, who persisted in shielding him, therefore the antagonistic party determined to act for themselves, and have him quickly put out of the way. On hearing this conversation, I at once started back to my camp, and sent one of my men off to the Colonel, to warn him not to take any notice of any message he received which recalled him, as any such message would be a deluding one. This course saved his life, for sure enough a day or two afterwards, messengers were sent to recall him in the King's name, but having been put on his guard by me he made some excuse for not going. This diabolical plan I managed to frustrate, before going home, without anyone but the intended victim and my messenger, knowing anything about it.

CHAPTER XI.

From this time the tone of Cetywayo towards the English Government began to change, and I could see, from the constant secret meetings which took place, that his intention was to make war somewhere, but I did not for a moment believe it was his intention to fight against the English, although I could see that he was greatly exasperated at the tone of the Government, assuming authority over him that he did not think they had a right to.

About this time I could perceive that there was a determination on the part of the English Government to make war with the Zulus, and to try and avert the evil, I wrote the following letter :—

E2

" *To the Aborigines Protection Society,*—

" I beg to write, for the information of your honourable
Society, and state that I am an Englishman by birth, and
have been a resident of the Zulu country, and living amongst
the Zulus, for the last twenty years, and I can confidently say
that there is no whiteman in this part of Africa so fitted to
judge of their feelings towards the English race as I am.

" I would not now address your honourable Society if
it were not that I have noticed a very strong, wrong, and
arbitrary feeling gaining ground against the Zulu nation on
the side of the white population in this part of South Africa.
A strong feeling of colour and jealousy I cannot understand,
unless it is on account of the independency of the Zulu race,
a feeling taken up without any just cause, and that feeling is
now on the verge of breaking out on the pretext of a false
claim of land boundary, a claim pretended to being upheld for
the Dutch Boers, who are no friends of the English race, and
are well known in this part of South Africa for their en-
croaching propensities, on any land belonging to the natives
of this country, to evade English laws, on the pretext of getting
permission to graze cattle, on the grass becoming scarce upon
their own farms, and afterwards claiming the land. A claim
in which the Natal Government have always upheld the
Zulus, and now, since the annexation of the Transvaal (in
1877), the head of the Government there, who professed
to side with the Zulus whilst he was in Natal, has now turned
round and claimed for the Dutch a country thickly inhabited
by the Zulus.

" I write this for the information of your honourable
Society, in the hope that you will try and put a stop to proceedings which will, if carried out, be the cause of bloodshed
in an unjust cause, as I can assure you that nothing but the

grossest acts of encroachment and oppression will cause the Zulus to take up arms against the English race, who wish to live at peace with them, not being ripe enough for civilisation or civilised laws.

"The standard rule that is gone by against the black races in this part of South Africa is the Amaxosa, or Cape Frontier Kafir, who is not to be compared to the Zulu, nothing but forced Christianity or civilisation will spoil the Zulu, and the class of foreign Missionaries we have in the country does more injury than good to them. Let them say what they like in their reports to the Societies, they make no convert to their faith, besides the pretended ones or vagabonds, who imagine that by being clothed and under the garb of Christianity they will be exempt from all King's service and laws of the country, and be allowed to roam about and do as they please.

" The Zulu nation, judiciously dealt with, would remain a firm ally and friend to the English, and it would be a shame for any false notions of power on the English side to take advantage of such power, and destroy the Zulu race, which would undoubtedly be the case if they were overthrown, they would then become a lot of bold rogues, and eventually give much trouble.

" One of the most unfair feautures in the case is this, that the head of the Transvaal Government (Sir T. Shepstone) has always advised Cetywayo to remain quiet, and not to go to war with the Boers in disputing the boundary, promising to see him righted, when, if it had been left to the Zulus and Boers themselves, I am sure the Boers would have got the worst of it. He now turns round, and is prepared to fight himself. when he knows he is only too well backed up by England for the Dutch, England not knowing the real facts.

"The Zulu acknowledge no individual title to land, permission only being given to squat, the land being looked on as belonging to the squatter only so long as he occupies it."

But before sending the above letter, I thought I would consult Mr. H. Escombe, and he advised me not to send the letter, as he had no doubt it was the intention of the English Government to disarm all the Native tribes in South Africa, and that I would only be making a fool of myself, or words to that effect, but at the same time advising me to await the arrival of Mr. J. Sanderson, who was editor of the *Natal Colonist*, a Colonial newspaper, now defunct, and who was expected out from England shortly. I acted on Mr. Escombe's advice, and on the arrival of Mr. Sanderson had a conversation with him, and gave him the letter. He pretended to think well of my proposal, but before he had time to carry it out, affairs, as regards Zulu matters, came to a crisis, and Mr. Sanderson died shortly afterwards, and so ended this matter.

In the earlier pages of this book I mentioned an incident connected with the illness of my son and the sacrifice of an ox, the termination of which served to strengthen the Zulus in their superstitious belief. I think it was in 1877 that a severe drought occurred, which lasted some months, and, after all the rain doctors had expended all their charms and devices, some of the Zulus persuaded the King to resort to the old custom of offering a sacrifice of oxen at the graves of the departed Kings. To this he at first demurred, being rather stingy with his cattle. At last he agreed, and a number of oxen—I think ten—were collected, and the principal old Indunas went with about two thousand men with these oxen to U'Pande's grave, and from there to the graves of the ancient Kings. Strange to say, they had not been gone an hour when, although there had been no sign of rain, the sky became overcast with heavy clouds, and as soon as they reached U'Pande's grave and solemnly commenced the deep and impressive National Chant, the rain began to descend, and continued for about a week. I was so much surprised at this that I wrote a letter to the *Colonist* stating the facts of the case, and saying that the thing would probably be stigmatised as heathenish superstition, but that if a congregation of whites had prayed in Church for rain, and it had descended from God in answer to their prayers, the matter would have been alluded to as an additional illustration of the wonderful efficacy of prayer. If this holds good with one, why not with the other ? They are both creatures of a Great Creator.

Matters now began to assume a very serious aspect, and not long after I arrived at my home—which, as I have said, was more than eighty miles from where the King resided— he again sent for me. Messengers were now constantly passing between Cetywayo and the Government, and reports began to be rife that a move was being made by the troops in Natal towards the borders. On my arrival at Maizekanye (meaning " Let it come—*i.e.*, the enemy—all at once—if it is determined on coming ") where the King was, I found that none of the head Indunas were there. After being with him a little while, and writing two letters—I think to the Natal Government—he wished me to write a letter conveying rather an angry message. This I refused to do, saying that I now plainly saw that it was his intention to quarrel with the English. I would not have anything more to do with his messages until Umnyamana and all the principal Indunas, including Uhamu, had come, as, in the event of an open rupture with the English, they would try to throw the blame on my shoulders. I further said that I did not believe he would have gone so far in sending word to the Governor with only Sirayo and Rabanina to advise him, as he knew they were

not recognised as Indunas of any position. After bandying
a few words with me, he acknowledged that I was right,
and next day he sent off to summon Umnyamana and the
others. I could now see he was in earnest, and intended to
fight, as I noticed a marked change in him, and I wrote to
that effect to the Governor of Natal. His manner towards
me became also quite changed, and he sent to me one morning
saying that as we two had the country to look after, and that
there were now so many reports, I had better leave and go
home, and watch what was going on in the lower part of the
country, and report everything to him, and he would likewise
report to me. This I could see was only an excuse to get me
out of the way. I sent back word to him to say that I would
go as soon as the Indunas Umnyamana, Uhamu, Sibepu, and
others had arrived, as I wished to talk to them first and explain to them the course I had taken. He did not say anything, but I could perceive he did not like my remaining. I
however waited until the Indunas arrived, and I explained to
them what had taken place, and that I refused to go further with
Cetywayo in sending messages to the Government with only
Sirayo and Rabanina as his advisers, as I could plainly see
they were leading him astray. A day or two after this, after
a meeting of all the headmen, about dusk one of the King's
servants came to me and warned me to fly, as Sirayo and
Rabanina had advised that I should be killed, as I would
report everything they said now that it was decided to fight
with the English. This I suspected was only a ruse to try
and frighten me away. I, however, that night slept with
my double-barrelled gun close beside me, determined, if
mischief was really their intention, not to fly, but settle a
couple before they killed me. However, all passed quietly off
that night. Next morning I made up my mind to go to
Cetywayo and tell him I knew everything that had been said

the day before, and that if he thought fit to kill me just for
giving him good advice, that I was not the only whiteman
on earth, and that he would find out his mistake before he
had finished. I said that my only reason for staying was my
desire to explain everything to Umnyamana and the Indunas,
but having done that, I was now ready to leave. I never in
my life saw a man look so ashamed of himself. He would
not look at me, but bent on one side, pretending to take
snuff. After remaining silent for some time, he spoke in a
very subdued voice. "Yes," he said, "you are right ; the
people look on you as a spy, and don't like your being here,
that is why I wanted you to leave, but now you have spoken
I want you to remain." This I refused to do, saying, "No,
now I can go, as I know that no one can blame me if anything goes wrong between you and the English." All this
time he was getting his soldiers up and marshalling them.
On the day after I had spoken to him he had two regiments
up before him in order to talk war, and lay wagers, and
challenge each other, as is their custom when preparing for
war. I had been sitting on a mound a short distance off
looking on, and being disgusted with the turn affairs were
now taking, I returned to camp and told my people to prepare, as I intended to start for home next day. From my
camp I could see the gathering, which broke up in an
unusual manner, as the soldiers shouted in an excited way,
and a great number left their usual course and came in the
direction of my camp. My people began to get very uneasy,
but I told them not to be alarmed but to remain sitting
quietly. The soldiers of the gathering came swarming past,
and several went right through my tents. On my speaking
to them they shouted out, "That is past (meaning my autho-
sity) ; a whiteman is nothing now in this country ; we will
stab him with an assegai and disembowel him." I had hard

work to keep my temper, but several of their captains, who
had come to me for a drink of water, and were sitting beside
me, persuaded me to keep quiet. That same evening I went
to bid Cetywayo farewell. He tried hard to persuade me to
remain, saying, " I am not a child ; I see the English wish
to have my country; but if they come in I will fight."   I
said, " Yes, I see, it is no use talking to you any more ; your
soldiers are leading you to a precipice over which you will go
headlong—*they* will turn back, and you will be pushed over
yourself." This forecast turned out to be too true, as he was
captured almost alone. Several Indunas and many of the
soldiers were not for war, as I understood from several private conversations with them. On one occasion Umnyamana
said to me, " What are you troubling yourself for any more ?
Cetywayo will not listen to what we say—leave him alone
and he will see what he will see." In a conversation I had
with Uhamu, he made use of words to the same effect.

CHAPTER XII.

On reaching my home, I sent several messengers to
Cetywayo in succession, trying to persuade him to relinquish
the idea of fighting with the English, but without effect.
In the meantime troops were being massed in Natal, and
were on their way to the border, and eventually I received a
message from Cetywayo, and also, at the same time, a letter
from the Secretary for Native Affairs, in answer to a letter of
mine begging him to inform me whether it was the intention
of the Government to make war, as, in such an event, I
should wish to quit the country or remain neutral. The
answer was that a message had been sent to Cetywayo telling
him to send some of his headmen to meet certain officials

despatched by His Excellency to convey to him the terms on which peace could be maintained, and requesting me to be present at the meeting. The message from Cetywayo was to the same effect, saying that the Indunas were coming, and requesting me to go with them. Accoringly a day was fixed and a meeting was held, as we all now know, at Tugela Drift, overlooked by what was afterwards named Fort Pearson, after Colonel Pearson of the Lower Column at Inyezane, &c., and the following Ultimatum was read to the Indunas, and then handed to them to convey to Cetywayo. They returned with me and slept at my lower station, Emangete, four miles or so from Tugela Drift (Ford). They tried to persuade me to accompany them back to Cetywayo in order that I might read the Ultimatum to him. Seeing that matters were coming to a crisis, I refused their request. They then left the written Ultimatum with me, and I have it now in my possession. The following is a true copy of it :—

"*Message from His Excellency the Lieutenant-Governor of Natal to Cetywayo, King of the Zulus, and Chief Men of the Zulu Nation.*

" The Lieutenant-Governor of Natal sends, in the name of the Queen's High Commissioner these further words to the Zulu King and Nation.

" These are the words of the High Commissioner, and they are sent by the Lieutenant-Governor through the same officers who delivered the words of the award in respect of the disputed boundary question, namely :—The Hon. John Wesley Shepstone, Secretary for Native Affairs, Natal : the Hon. Charles Brownlee, Resident Commissioner for Native Affairs in the Cape Colony, at present attached to the Staff of the High commissioner : Mr. Henry Francis Fynn, Resident Magistrate, Umsinga Division, Natal : and Colonel

Forester Walker, of Her Majesty's Scots Guards, lately attached to the Staff of the High Commissioner ; to be delivered
by them to the Zulu representatives, that they may be duly
communicated to the King and Council and people of the
Zulu Nation.

" The King and nation will recognise in the award that
has just been given on the matter of the disputed boundary,
the determination of the British Government to give effect to
the words which have been spoken at different times by its
representatives in this country regarding the matter.

" The dispute respecting the boundary was one that had
existed for many years. It was a question between the Government of the Transvaal Republic and the Zulu nation.
The latter made many and frequent representations to the
Natal Government on the subject. The Government of Natal
was always anxious that the dispute should be settled by
peaceful means, and always counselled the Zulu King accordingly. It considered that the dispute might be and could
be settled properly and satisfactorily, by means of an
impartial inquiry ; and was always ready to use its good
offices for that purpose. The opportunity for doing so, however, did not occur. The years passed without any settlement of the question, and at length last year the Transvaal
came under British rule. Now when that took place, the
Zulu King, if he trusted the British Government, had every
reason to believe that whatever rights the Zulus might have in
the disputed territory, would be investigated and accorded to
them. But, without waiting, the King sent armed Zulus
on to the disputed territory, and by threats obliged the European settlers in it to leave their homes. This proceeding on
the part of the Zulu King might well have been resented by
the English Government ; but having regard to the promises
and words of its representatives in times past, and desirous

to avoid all appearance of prejudging a long standing question in which its own interests had become involved, it withheld its hand in order that the inquiry so long spoken of might be held.

" The inquiry was instituted by the Government of Natal, and was held by trust persons appointed by the Lieutenant-Governor of Natal. It was held in the presence of the representatives both of the Transvaal Government and the Zulu King and nation, and all that was said and put forward in support of these claims by both parties was heard and considered.

" It is clear from the enquiry that some negotiations took place between Cetywayo and the Boers in 1861. Cetywayo's right of succession to the late King Panda was then very uncertain. Two other sons of Panda were in the hands of the Boers, and the evidence goes to show that certain promises to cede land were made by Cetywayo, partly in order to obtain the surrender of these two sons of Panda, and partly in consideration of presents of cattle.

" What was the extent and character of the promises made by Cetywayo has been since disputed, but promises of some sort there undoubtedly were. Certain land was also beaconed off, but no recognition or confirmation of the cessions said to have been promised by Cetywayo appears ever to have been given by the King Panda, or by the great Council of the Zulus, and accordingly the Commissioners who inquired into the dispute, after careful deliberation, recorded their finding against any authoritative or sufficient cession of that land having been made by he King or nation. This decision has been accepted by the High Commissioner, and has now been communicated to the Zulu King and nation. This award assigns as belonging to the Zulu nation, and as subject

to the Zulu King, a great portion of the disputed land claimed
by the King, which lies between the Buffalo and Pongola
Rivers.

"But whilst the British Government in this way gives
up to the Zulu King and nation land which is thought by the
Commissioners to be by strict right belonging to the Zulus,
and whilst the British Government has, and always will have,
a due regard for it, at the same time, will strictly require all
that is due to its own honours and the just rights and interests
of the Queen's subjects.

"It has already been intimated in connection with the
award, which was an award regarding the territory lying on
this, or the south side of the Pongola River, that on the
other, or north side of that river, the Zulu King must not, as
he has of late appeared inclined to do, attempt to take any
action in respect of that territory, as if he had any right or
jurisdiction there, but that if the King has, or thinks he has,
any claims of any nature in that direction, he must state them
to the British Government, by whom they will be duly
considered.

"The High Commissioner has had under his consideration
the proceedings connected with the outrage that was committed some months ago in Natal territory by Zulu subjects,
the sons, relatives, and people of the Zulu Chief Sirayo. This
has been a grievous and gross outrage committed on British
territory.   Mehlokazulu, Inkumbokazulu, and Tyekwana, sons
of Sirayo, and Zuluhlenya, a brother of Sirayo, with a large
number of armed attendants, crossed the Buffalo River into
Natal territory in two parties, and by force and violence took
out of Natal territory two Zulu women.   Having taken these
woman back into the Zulu country, they there, as is reported,
killed them.

" The Lieutenant-Governor of Natal, when he heard of these occurrences, sent messages, one on the 1st and another on the 16th of August, to the King, stating what had occurred, and requesting that the sons and relatives of Sirayo, the ringleaders of the outrages, should be given up to the Natal Government for punishment for the offences committed by them in Natal territory. Cetywayo, in reply, admitted that Sirayo's people had done wrong, but he has endeavoured to make light of the offence, and he has not given up the men as desired. Instead of doing this they sent £50, which he wished the Natal Government to accept as a fine in lieu of the punishment of Sirayo's people. The money was not accepted, and the King was told that such a fine would be no punishment for those guilty of the offence, and no reparation for the outrage. The King said, however, that he would lay the matter and the demand of the Lieutenant-Governor before his great Council ; but many weeks have passed and no further intimation has been received by the Natal Government to show that the King has laid the matter before the Council, or what the deliberations of the Council has been.

" Her Majesty's High Commissioner has now therefore to require that the Zulu King will forthwith send in to the Natal Government, for trial under the laws of the Colony, for the offence committed by them in the Colony, the persons of Mehlokazulu, Inkumbokazulu, and Tyekwana, the sons of Sirayo and also Zuluhlenza, the brother of Sirayo, who was wrongly accused, as he was not one of the party who came into Natal territory, but was at Umhlan-den-Hlorn at the time, he is accordingly exempted from this demand, but the others now demanded must be sent in and delivered over to the Natal Authorities within twenty days from the date that this demand is made. The Zulu King is required in addition, to pay to the British Government, a fine of 500 head of cattle for the outrage, and for his delay in complying with the request of the Natal Government. These cattle must also be sent in within the period above named.

"There has also been another offence committed by Zulu subjects, on the persons of British subjects at Middle Drift on the Tugela River, below Fort Buckingham. These two British subjects, Messieurs Smith and Deighton were, whilst at or near the drift in the month of September last, surrounded by a party of fifteen Zulus, who, armed with guns and assegais, in an excited state, took hold of the two white men, and made them sit down, demanding what they were doing there, as the ground belonged to Cetywayo. Gradually the Zulus became more quiet, and after detaining the two white men for an hour and a-half, or thereabouts, they allowed them to go. This interference with and treatment of two British subjects was an interference and treatment which was unwarrantable. It was an offence against the persons of two British subjects which cannot be passed over without notice, and as a punishment for the offence and a warning against the commission of similar offences in future, the High Commissioner requires that a fine of 100 head of cattle shall be paid to the British Government. This fine must also be paid within the period of twenty days from the date of the communication being made.

"The two cases referred to have been cases of offence—one of them of a most serious and outrageous nature—committed by individual Zulu subjects in British Territory, or against the persons of British subjects for which it has been found necessary to demand that reparation shall be made in the manner above stated.

"There is also the case of Umbelini, a Swazi refugee living in the Zulu Country, who is charged with having recently made a murderous raid into the country north of the

Pongolo, which is claimed as British territory by the Transvaal Government. It will be necessary for the offenders in this case to be given up to be tried by the Transvaal Courts for the offence of which they have been accused, and a further communication will be made to Cetywayo when the Transvaal Government has stated who, besides Umbelini, must be given up to be tried.

" But beyond these matters which relate to certain offences committed by certain Zulu subjects against the British Government, the attention of Her Majesty's Commissioner has of necessity been given to the state of Government and the state of affairs in the Zulu Country, as affecting both the conditions of the Zulu people, and the peace and safety of the Queen's dominions lying adjacent to Zululand, and of other tribes and peoples, the allies or friendly neighbours of the British Government.

" In the time of the late King Panda the relations of the British Government and the Zulus had always been of a friendly nature. The English Government and the Zulus were near neighbours, and all the Zulu nation can bear witness that the English Government never did anything unfriendly or showed in any way otherwise than most friendly and well disposed towards the Zulus. Panda, it is well known, was established in the chieftainship by the Dutch Emigrant Farmers, who defeated the Zulu King Dingaan. It was after this that the English came into Natal, and established relations with Panda and the Zulu nation.

" Panda's reign was a more peaceful one than those of his predecessors, and his rule was milder and more tolerant. He encouraged trade. He allowed Christian Missionaries to settle in the land, and set aside stations for them and gave them land, and there was good promise of an improvement in the condition of the Zulu people.

F

" Unhappily, during the latter part of his reign, and when he became old, trouble came upon the land in consequence of the difference between Cetywayo and his brothers as to who should be successor to the King.

" Panda had always behaved in a loyal and friendly manner to the British Government, and, when on account of the continued excitement and uneasiness in the Zulu country, he asked the Government of Natal to interfere, the Government sent Mr. Shepstone, the Secretary for Native Affairs, to recommend Panda to nominate a successor, and so remove the uncertainty on that point, and the cause of dispute among the brothers. The result was the nomination of the house of Cetywayo, which, settling the dispute of succession, gave quiet again to the Zulu country.

" After the death of Panda, the sons of the late King, and the head men of the Zulu nation, assembled and sent messengers to the Government of Natal, saying that the nation found itself wandering because of the death of the King. " There was no King," they said, and the messengers brought from the nation four oxen, representing the " Head of the King," to the Natal Government. They further asked that Mr. Shepstone, who had been present at the nomination of Cetywayo, might go and establish what was wanted, and, at the same time, breathe the spirit by which the nation should be governed. They said, moreover, it was the will of the nation that the new King should be the son of the British Government.

" The Government of Natal had no wish to mix itself up with these arrangements of the Zulu people ; but eventually it consented, and sent Mr. Shepstone to take part in the installation. It was the wish of Cetywayo that this should be done—it was the wish of the whole Zulu nation. In con-

senting to this, the British Government had no selfish object
of any kind. It did not seek to obtain a single foot of land
for itself, nor any advantage nor any privilege whatever. It
wanted nothing for itself, and demanded nothing for itself.
Its only motive in complying with the wish of the Zulu nation
and in taking part in the coronation of the new King was
that in doing so it might help to assure the peace of
the Zulu country, and promote in some degree the welfare of
the Zulu people.

" In taking part, therefore, the only conditions it made
were in favour of the good government of the people. At a
formal meeting held previous to the installation between Mr.
Shepstone, Cetywayo, and the headmen of the Zulu nation,
several matters were discussed, chief among which were
certain regulations or laws for the better government of the
Zulu people, which were to be proclaimed on the occasion of
the installation. Subsequently, on the day of the installation,
the laws were formally proclaimed by Mr. Shepstone.

" It was proclaimed—

(1) That the indiscriminate shedding of blood should
cease in the land.

(2) That no Zulu should be condemned without open
trial, and the public examination of witnesses, for
and against, and that he should have the right of
appeal to the King.

(3) That no Zulu's life should be taken without the
previous knowledge and consent of the King,
after such trial has taken place, and the right of
appeal had been allowed to be exercised.

(4) That for minor crimes, the loss of property, all or
a portion, should be substituted for the punishment of death.

F2

" Now, these laws were formally proclaimed by Mr. Shepstone, who represented the British Government in Natal, and proclaimed with the formal consent of Cetywayo, of the chief men of the nation, and of the natives there assembled. It was not done as a mere idle ceremony or form ; it was not done in secret, but in public ; it was not done in the dark, but in the open day ; it was not done in solitude, but at the Royal Kraal, in the presence and the hearing of the King, the Chiefs, and the assembled people. They were laws for the good government of the Zulu people. The subject of them had been carefully and deliberately discussed beforehand between the British representatives and Cetywayo and his Councillors, and agreed upon, and then afterwards, in the hearing and presence of the people, the laws had been solemnly affirmed.

" These laws for the well-being of the Zulu people were the conditions required by the British Government in return for the countenance and support given by it to the new Zulu King, by the presence of its representation, and by his taking part in the King's coronation ; and once spoken as they were, they cannot be broken without compromising the dignity, the good faith, and the honour of the British Government.

" The British Government now asks, how has it been in this matter ? Have the promises then made been kept ? Have the laws which were then proclaimed been observed ? Let the Zulu King answer !

" There is but one answer. The King and people know very well that the promises have not been kept. They know that these laws have not been observed, but that they have been broken time after time, and that they are almost daily broken in the Zulu country. They know very well that the lives of hundreds of Zulu people—men, women, old and young—have been taken since that day without any trial at all, that the indiscriminate shedding of blood has not ceased, and that the killing of Zulu people has gone on as if no promise had ever been made, and no law ever proclaimed.

" Hence it is that all Zulus live in fear to lose their lives any day. No man knows when he may be suddenly set upon and killed, and all belonging to him destroyed or taken away.

" How can these things be? Were the words which were spoken at the coronation mere empty words, meaning nothing? The Zulu King knows that it is not so, and that it cannot be so. The British Government in Natal did not want, and it did not ask to take any part in the installation of Panda's successor. It wished well to the Zulu country and the Zulu people, but for itself it wished for nothing, it asked for nothing. It was Cetywayo himself. It was the Zulu nation assembled together that sent to the Government to ask it to take part. Even then the Government did not desire to take part in what was being done, but it consented to do so, asking nothing for itself, but asking certain conditions for the good of the Zulu people.

" The conditions which it asked were conditions for the protection of the lives of the Zulu people, that they might not be condemned and slain without trial, without knowing what their offence was, without cause, and without chance of justice. These were the laws proclaimed.

" The British Government cannot, then, allow that the words which were once spoken on its part should be empty words, or that the promises which were made to it, and for which it became the mouthpiece and the guarantee to the whole Zulu nation, should be treated as if they were mere idleness and empty sound. But for five years they have been so treated, and now it can be no longer so.

" The promises have not been kept, and how is it possible
they can be kept so long as the present system of Government is maintained by the King?

" The present system of Government is destroying the
country. All the young men, all the able-bodied men of the
country, are taken as soldiers. They are taken from their
homes at an age when they are becoming useful to their
parents, and are kept for several years in the compulsory
service of the King. They are not allowed to marry, as the
other men around them, as in Natal, as among the Amaswazi,
as among the Amapondo. They cannot marry when they
desire to do so, but they must await the permission of the
King, and they are often kept for seven years without the
permission to do so. They are not allowed to labour for
themselves, or to plant, or to reap, or to live in quiet and
in peace with their families and relatives. They are constantly summoned up to the King's kraals, as if for war,
although there is no enemy to fight with, and thus they come
to fight amongst themselves, and blood is shed, and there is
distress and moaning in the land ; or they are sent out in
parties to surround the kraals of those who have given offence
to the King, or who are accused by private enemies, and who
then, without trial and without a word, are killed, their kraals
laid desolate, and their families, and all they have, carried off
and destroyed.

" Thus the army is made an instrument, not for the defence of the country, but for the oppression of the people.
All the best interests of the Zulu Country and the happiness
of the Zulu people are sacrificed in order that the King may
keep up this large army. For what purpose is this army kept
up ? Is there an enemy ? Where is the enemy ? Cetywayo
knows very well that there is no enemy, and that there is no
occasion for this large army. In the days of Chaka or

Dingaan it might be different, but now on all sides of the Zulu Country is the territory of the British Government, or of its allies and friendly neighbours. The King knows very well that the British Government is a peaceful and friendly power, and that it wishes well to the Zulu people, and that it wishes them to live in peace and comfort. The King knows this well, for did not his father live to become an old man under the shelter of the British Government, and has not Cetywayo himself grown up to manhood under the eye of the English?

" With regard to the neighbouring native tribes, the Basuto, Amapondo, the Amaswazi, and others, they are either the subjects or the allies or neighbours of the British Government, and the Zulu King knows he has nothing to fear from them. They are, besides, peaceful people and not given to war and aggression.

" For what purpose then does the Zulu King keep up this large army, which brings so much hardship and so much misery upon the Zulu people themselves? It can serve no good purpose. It can be made of no use, except it be used for the oppression of the Zulu people or for aggression upon British subjects or the allies and neighbours of the British Government.

" There is, therefore, no real need for the army. The present system is working the destruction of the Zulu people. The army was used against the very people of the country to which it belongs. It is the strength of the nation destroying the nation itself.

" Let the nation say if this is not so? Besides, while the King keeps up this army, whilst he is constantly calling it together, it is impossible for his neighbours to feel secure.

They never know what may happen, and the British Government is obliged to keep large numbers of the Queen's troops in Natal and the Transvaal in order to protect British subjects against the dangers of a possible aggression by the Zulu King.

"This state of things cannot last. It is dangerous to the peace of all the countries adjoining Zululand, and it is hurtful to the Zulu people themselves. The British Government cannot allow it to continue. It has become absolutely necessary that some change should be made.

" It is necessary that the military system which is at present kept up by the King should be done away with, as a bad and hurtful one, and that he should instead adopt such military regulations as may be decided on after consultation with the great Council of the Zulus, and with the representatives of the British Government.

" It is necessary that the Zulu army, as it is now, shall be disbanded, and that the men shall return to their homes.

" Let the obligation on every able-bodied man to come out for the defence of his country, when it is needed, remain, but until then let it be that every man shall live, if he pleases, quietly at his own home.

" Let every man then be free to remain at his home, and let him plant and sow, and reap and tend his cattle, and let him live in peace and with his family.

" Let him not be called out for war or for fighting, or for assembling in regiments, except with the permission of the great Council of the nation assembled, and with the consent also of the British Government.

" Let every man, when he comes to man's estate, be free to marry. Let him not wait for years before he gets permission to do this, for oftentimes the King forgets to give the permission, and the years pass on and the man becomes old. But let him be free to marry when he pleases, as it is in Natal.

" So will the King have contented subjects.

" Then with respect to the promises made at the coronation, let rules at once be laid down that any Zulu, man or woman, old or young, who is accused of any crime, be tried by properly appointed Indunas before punishment, that no one may be punished without cause, and that the life of no one be taken until the offence of which he is accused be heard openly against him, and on answers given by him in defence, in order that those by whom he is tried may say whether he is guilty or not before he is punished ; and if anyone is declared guilty let him not be killed until the King has given his consent, and until the person declared guilty has been able to make an appeal to the King.

" Thus it was promised it should be at the time of the coronation, but the promises have not been kept.

" But in future it will be necessary that the promises be kept, for the British Government holds itself bound to see that this is so, and in order that they may be kept and that the laws regarding them may be duly carried out, the Queen's High Commissioner, on behalf of the British Government, will appoint an officer as his deputy to reside in the Zulu country, or on its immediate borders, who will be the eyes, and ears, and mouth of the British Government towards the Zulu King and the great Council of the nation.

" What words the King or the Council of the nation may desire to say to the British Government can then be said through this officer, as also what words the British Government may desire to say to the King and the great Council can be said through him, so that all misunderstandings and questions that arise between the two countries, or between the subjects of the two countries, may be dealt with and settled through this one officer speaking with the King and the great Council.

" This officer will see that the rules regarding the trials of all Zulus before punishment are kept, and that no man is killed without trial, but that all men may have an opportunity of answering the accusations brought against them, and if need be, of appealing to the King.

" He will see also that the arrangements to be made regarding the army are carried out; that no one is called out for war without necessity; that all men are allowed to live at their homes in peace; and that every young man is free to marry. So will it be well with the Zulu people.

" The late King Panda allowed several European missionaries to settle in Zululand. Cetywayo also allowed them to stay in the country, but during the last two years some of the natives living on the Mission Stations were killed without trial, or form of trial, and others were terrified, and thus the missionaries have, most of them, been obliged to abandon their stations, and the High Commissioner desires that all those missionaries who, until the last year, lived in the Zulu country and occupied stations, as also the natives belonging to the stations, be allowed to return and occupy their stations. He desires also that all missionaries be allowed to teach as in Panda's time, and that no Zulu shall be punished for listening to them. If any Zulu wishes, of his own choice, to listen to the missionary he is free to do so. If any native living on a Mission Station does wrong, he will be liable to punishment, but he must be tried first.

" If any case of dispute occurs in which any of the missionaries, or in which any European is concerned, such dispute should be heard by the King in public and in the presence of the British Resident ; and no sentence of expulsion from Zululand shall be carried out until it has been communicated by the King to the Resident, and until it has been approved by the Resident.

" These are the words of Her Majesty's High Commissioner, which the Lieutenant-Governor of Natal sends to the Zulu King and the chief men of the nation, and for the whole Zulu Nation.

" These are the conditions which Her Majesty's High Commissioner, in the name of the British Government, considers necessary for the establishment of a satisfactory state of things in the Zulu country, and for the peace and safety of the adjoining countries. Let, therefore, the King and the chief men of the nation consider them, and let them give their answer regarding them within 30 days from the day on which this communication is made to the Zulu representatives, in order that Her Majesty's High Commissioner may then know if the King and the great Council agrees to the words which are here given, and will give effect to these conditions, which are necessary both for the peace and safety of the Queen's subjects and allies and also for the safety and the welfare of the Zulu people, to which the Queen's Government wishes well.

" (Signed) HENRY BULWER,
" Lieutenant-Governor."

CHAPTER XIII.

Although the Ultimatum alluded to in the last chapter never reached Cetywayo, but was left at my place at Emengete—about four miles from the Tugela—I nevertheless despatched one of my own men to the Zulu King, conveying through him the full purport of the document, as I felt convinced that his own messengers would not tell him one-half of it. My men arrived some days before the King's own messengers reached him, and brought back a message from Cetywayo, complaining of the short time given to collect the cattle demanded, and at the same time sent another message to me, saying that if it came to fighting I was to stand on one side. I wrote a letter to the Natal Government stating the King's complaint as to the shortness of the time given to collect the cattle, and received the following reply :—

" Office of Secretary for Native Affairs, Natal,
" 26th December, 1878.

" To JOHN R. DUNN, Zulu Country.

" SIR,—I have the honour to acknowledge the receipt of your letter of the 18th instant, which the Lieut.-Governor has laid before His Excellency the High Commissioner for his information.

" I am directed to express the satisfaction of the High Commissioner at the receipt of your letter, and to inform you that the word of the Government, as already given, cannot be altered.

" Unless the prisoners and cattle are given up within the time specified Her Majesty's troops will advance, but, in consideration of the disposition expressed in your letter to comply with the demands of the Government, the troops will be halted at convenient posts within the Zulu border, and will await the expiration of the term of 30 days, without in the meantime taking any hostile action, unless it is provoked by the Zulus.

" (Signed)   J. W. SHEPSTONE,
" Acting Secretary for Native Affairs."

About the time of the above date, Lord Chelmsford and Commodore Sullivan came up to the Tugela, and so I crossed that river and requested an interview with them, which was granted.

In course of the conversation Lord Chelmsford asked me what course—in the present aspect of affairs—I intended to take? I told him that my intention was to remain neutral. To this he answered, "I cannot allow you to do that. You must either take one side or the other—join us, or take the consequences." I told him that I had no quarrel with the Zulus, and did not like taking up arms against them, but begged him to advise me what to do. After considering for a little while, he said, "Take my advice, Mr. Dunn, and cross over to this side of the river (the southern boundary of Zululand) with all your people, and bring as many more with you as you can. We will give you room to locate them, and will feed them free of expense to you ; and after the war is over I promise to see you reinstated in your possessions." For this advice I thanked him, and promised to act on it. Up to this time I did not believe that matters would culminate in war, but now I could see that it was not to be avoided.

Lord Chelmsford said he was afraid that he would not get the Zulus to fight. But, from my experience, I knew that if the fighting die was once cast, Cetywayo would concentrate his forces, and risking everything on one great battle, fall upon the column that he thought would give him most trouble, so I advised Lord Chelmsford to divide his forces into two strong columns, so that either would be strong enough to cope with the whole of the Zulu army. Lord Chelmsford laughed at this idea, and said, "The only thing I am afraid of is that I won't get Cetywayo to fight." I said, "Well, my lord, supposing you get to his kraal, and he won't fight, what will you do?" His answer was, "I must drive him into a corner, and make him fight."

I asked the above question, as I had begged Cetywayo
not to fight, even if the English army invaded his kraal.

I felt sure that no real grounds for war—beyond an
unreasonable dread on the part of the public of the Zulus—
existed, hence my advice to Cetywayo.

I must not forget to mention that, before meeting Lord
Chelmsford, I had written to the Natal Government, impress-
ing upon them the imperative necessity of sending two very
strong columns into Zululand if war was once entered on, as
I felt sure Cetywayo would try to take them in succession,
and I also knew that if the Zulus were properly met at the
start, and were defeated, the war would very soon be over.
But Sir Bartle Frere and Lord Chelmsford much underrated
the Zulus, and hence the disaster at Isandhlwane and the pro-
longed war. Whereas, as I say, if the Zulus had been
properly met at first, the war would have been over in two
months, and the best of terms made.

My people all this time were in a great state of perplexity,
as they were at a loss as to my intentions, for I had not
devulged them to anyone beyond leading my people to believe
that I was going to take them coastwards out of the way.
But on the 30th of December, 1878, I gave notice to all my
people at the Ungoye (about 35 miles from the Tugela River)
to collect bag and baggage and join me, the time being opportune, as most of Cetywayo's men—who might have interfered with mine—had gone up to the King's kraal to attend
the Feast of First Fruits. My people, with their cattle, got
down safely the next morning to Emangete, from which
place I went on to the Tugela. The latter river was full, and
the scene can be imagined. The river and its banks were
crowded with thousands of natives and cattle—I had three
thousand head of my own—and the lowing, or rather bellow-

ing, of the cows and calves, the bleating of sheep, goats, &c., the crying of babies, blended with the shoutings of women, made a perfect babel of confusion. However, with the kind assistance of the Naval Brigade, I managed to get all safely across the river in two days, but the discomfort of the first night on the Natal side I shall never forget. Before I could get shelter for my family, a cold rain set in, and so everything was wet and miserable, and it was only owing to the perseverance of my cooks that we got anything to eat; my people meanwhile shifting for themselves amongst the bushes, &c. When my people arrived on the Natal side of the river they were deprived of all the guns they had, which were mine, and which were given to the Native Police for the defence of the border. For this loss I was never compensated.

The next day being fine was passed in drying and getting ready to start, which was effected during the course of the day, my people and cattle going on to a site selected for my location near the Border Agency. The next day I followed with my family. My natives, I must say, before leaving the river were very much disheartened on seeing what they they thought was the whole force of whites, and I had hard work to dissuade many of them from going back to Zululand, and throwing in their lot with the Zulus. However the arrival of more troops gave them fresh confidence.

The spot I was located on turned out to be a very unhealthy one for both people and cattle. Hardly a day passed without some deaths occurring among my people, and during the time I was there I lost three hundred of my cattle, but I was fortunate enough to sell a considerable number to the Government at a very good price.

Lord Chelmsford broke his promise as to feeding my people and I had to do so myself at a very heavy expense,

having to kill cattle for them and supply them with mealies
which were only to be had in any quantity from the Government, who parted with them as a favour and at a high price.
Fortunately I had wagons and oxen at my disposal, and I
could send to D'Urban for supplies, otherwise the expense of
transport, which was, at that time, very high, would have
been very heavy. While I was staying at this place, and
shortly after the Isandhlwane disaster had happened, an
amusing false alarm occurred. One evening I had just
finished my dinner when I heard a cannonading going on at
the Lower Tugela Drift, where the troops were stationed. I
was then living about three hundred yards from the Border
Agency Station. I jumped up and at once went over there,
knowing that, the river being in flood, if there was an attack
by Zulus at all, and it must be on the further bank of the
stream, at Fort Tenedos, where the Naval Brigade was
stationed, as I felt sure the Zulus would not cross the river in
the dark. On reaching the hut of the Border Agent, I found
his horse, ready saddled, standing outside, and on entering his
hut I found him fumbling among some things. He was
ready booted and spurred. On my asking him what he was
doing, he said—handing me a pistol—" Good God ! where is
your horse ! let's be off to a place of safety, don't you hear ?
the Zulus must be across." I said, " What? and leave my
people to look after themselves ? No, I won't do that ; where
are my guns that you took from my people ? let me have
them back, I will not leave." I then told a couple of men,
who were with me, to shout out the call of my tribe, and
within ten minutes I had all my men with me eagerly calling
out to be armed. I asked the Border Agent to give me out
the arms, at the same time asking him if he had sent out in
the direction of the firing to see what was wrong ? He said
he had not done so. He then went, with me, and opened a

a place he called his magazine, where my guns were supposed
to be, I, in the meantime, having sent some of my own men
to run and ascertain the cause of alarm. On his opening the
" magazine " only about a dozen guns were there, and none
of those mine. He only then recollected that my guns had
been given to the Native Police. Anyone in my (then) position can imagine my feelings, and I could not help making
use of a strong expression, saying, " Here are my men, who
really could be of some service, hemmed in like a lot of old
women with nothing to defend themselves or families with."
Whilst I was looking over the guns to see if I could select a
serviceable one, the Border Agent said to me, " Dunn, will
you take charge ? I am off to give the alarm." The firing,
by this time, had ceased, and away he went. His own police
were very much disgusted with his leaving them without any
orders. He had not been away half-an-hour, when my men
who I sent to learn the cause of alarm, returned, saying that
the affair was a false alarm which had occurred on the further
side of the river.

I at once sent off a man to Mr. Jackson, the Magistrate,
at Stanger (to where the Border Agent had gone) with a
short note stating that the alarm was a false one, and that
there was no danger at all. The troubles of the Border
Agent, however, were not over. In taking a short cut to get
into the main road, he had to go through a cane field. The
night was very dark and a drizzling rain was falling. Just
as he got on to a slippery siding, he heard a number of
Coolies, who had taken the alarm, jabbering, shouting and
making night hideous, and having Zulu on the brain himself,
he turned his horse to fly, when the animal lost his footing,
and great was the fall. In the scrimmage up he lost his
spurs, and was altogether in a deplorable plight, scared,
covered with mud, wet, and miserable. He told me the tale
G

himself, acknowledging that he was in a great fright, as, he said, he was no fighting man, and had a great dread of having an assegai sticking in him. The man I sent reached Stanger, and found that the alarm had already been given, and all the people about were going into laager. My note, however, re-assured them and they returned to their homes next morning.

At daylight, on the ensuing day, it was found that the only damage done by the cannonading of the Marines was a dead horse and a battered bag of mealies, both of which were riddled with bullets. Thus ended this farce.

The crossing of the troops into Zululand, and the march to Etshowe, I will leave to others to describe, but after Isandhlwane, the Colony was in a constant state of alarm.

Chapter XIV.

Some time after the happening of the events, as above described, when I was on my way back from D'Urban, and when I was at the Umhlali Hotel, I received a note from the late Mr. Reynolds, saying that Lord Chelmsford was at his place, and would very much like to see me. So the next morning, about nine o'clack, I started in compliance with his wishes, but met the General—who had also started to see me—on the road. He got off his horse and asked me to allow him to get into my trap. while my groom, who was with me, could ride his horse, as he wanted to have some private conversation with me. I then turned back and drove him part of his way on his journey. We had a long conversation, the purport of which was that he had been greatly mislead by people who knew nothing of Zululand or the Zulus, and that he would be glad if I would

give him my advice and assistance. I promised to raise a
body of one hundred and fifty of my own men to act as
scouts and hand them over to the officers in command of the
Forces at the Tugela, which I did as soon as I got back to
where I was staying. These men that I raised were attached
to Major Barrow's Horse, and did good service.

The force at the Etshowe was now entirely cut off, and
no communication could be had with them, and I was again
asked for assistance, and high reward offered if I could get
anyone I could depend on to run despatches to the besieged.
This I succeeded in doing, as I started two men at dark, who
went right through during the night, reaching Etshowe at
daybreak. The first time they met with no adventure, but
the second time they walked right in amongst a lot of Zulus,
who were on the watch. They were chased, and several shots
fired at them, but, the night being dark, they escaped. On
the last occasion, however, they were again chased, and one
of them—the one who had the despatches—was killed. Lord
Chelmsford promised that these messengers should be
rewarded, and the relatives of the man who had lost his life
compensated. But nothing came of it, beyond what I paid
myself and a couple of sovereigns given by the Rev. Robert-
son. So much for the word of anyone representing the
authority of a military Government. In the first place, I had
to pay for all the food I got from the Government at a much
higher rate than I could have bought it for privately, and
this supply, which was granted as a great favour, was so in-
sufficient that I had to keep on killing cattle for my people.
In the second place my despatch-runners, one of whom, as I
have said, was killed, got no reward ; and in the third place
I had, to suit political purposes, been appointed a Chief, and
after all was over, was quietly told to resume my old position
which was simply an impossibility.

G2

Some little while after I had supplied my men to act as scouts, the detachment entrenched at Etshowe under Colonel Pearson proclaimed that they were running short of provisions, and could not hold out beyond a certain time, so, as we know, a relief column was organised under Lord Chelmsford himself. He asked me to put down in writing what I thought the duty of the scouts to be.   This I did, and sent him the writing, in reply to which I received the following letter :—

" Lower Tugela, 25th March, 1879.

" Dear Mr. Dunn,—

" I am much obliged to you for your suggestions regarding the employment of your men as scouts, which will be carried out.

" I think it will be very advantageous if you yourself were to accompany me as far as the Inyezani River.   I would not ask you to go further.   Your presence with me would ensure the efficient scouting of your men, and I feel sure that I should myself derive much assistance from your experience of Zulu warfare and from your knowledge of the country passed through.

" I quite understand that you do not feel justified in running the risk of depriving those who look to you for support of your helping hand, but I do not think that what I ask you to do entails any particular risk.   Awaiting your reply,

"I remain,
" Faithfully yours,
" (Signed)   CHELMSFORD."

" I should not of course ask you to do any work with the scouts, but simply to accompany me as an adviser."

" C."

" I shall probably start the day after to-morrow."

Lord Chelmsford backed up the foregoing letter by send-iny one of his staff to induce me to comply. However, I replied to neither letter or message, but rode over next morn-ing and had an interview with the General. After a long talk, during which I explained to him my reason for not wishing to join against the Zulus, he said, " Well, Mr. Dunn, I feel sure you can be of much service to me, which, if you will render, you will receive the thanks of Her Majesty's Go-vernment, to say nothing of my own personally, but if you do not, you know what will be thought of you for withholding the assistance you can give, and you can expect nothing after the war is over." I then asked him to allow me until next morning to consider, which he did, On reaching home, I began to think earnestly of the situation. I could see that I could be of service in pointing out the means of averting another disaster, and besides, I knew that in the fighting be-tween the Boers and the English at the Bay (D'Urban) my father had suffered by remaining neutral, so I made up my mind to go with Lord Chelmsford to the relief of the Etshowe garrison. The next morning I rode over and conveyed my decision to the General, at which he was very much pleased.

A few days afterwards a start was made, and at the end of the fourth day we had done a distance of about eighteen miles and I selected a good position for the Ginginhlovu camp, as I felt sure there was a strong force of Zulus in the neighbourhood, and I did not like the idea of being caught on the line of march with men of whom I knew nothing— martially or otherwise. Shortly after we formed laager at Ginginhlovu a heavy thunder shower fell, which drenched everything. As soon as it was over Lord Chelmsford asked me to go out with him to reconnoitre. This we did, but found the Inyezani river so full from the heavy rains that we could not cross. On our way back to camp I saw several small columns of smoke rising here and there in the vicinity, and I was at once convinced that they arose from the Zulu camp, and told Lord Chelmsford so, and advised that mounted men should be sent next morning to draw them on to an attack *before* we broke camp for a forward march. This he agreed to. On our return to camp we found everything in a pretty mess of slush and mud in general. Tents there were none, and so we had to pick out the driest spots under the wagons, the General doing the same as the others. There was no distinction, and so no grumbling, and we were all most thankful for something to eat.

The next morning, about daybreak, there was a call to arms, and shouts of " There they are ! " and, sure enough, on my getting up on to a wagon, I could see dense masses of Zulus coming down on to us, and trying—with their usual tactics—to encircle us. When they came to within about fifteen hundred yards, the order was given to fire. I got on a buck wagon—*i.e.*, a wagon without a tent—with my rifle. This was an ammunition wagon. I reserved my fire until the Zulus got within three hundred yards, and when I was picking off my men at that range, I noticed that the bullets of the volleys fired by the soldiers were striking the ground a long way beyond their mark, and on looking at their rifles I found that they still had the long range sights up, and that they were firing wildly in any direction. I then called to Lord Chelmsford, asking him to give orders for lowering the sights. This was done, and the soldiers began to drop the enemy faster and consequently, check the advance, but again, when I had my sight down to one hundred yards—as the Zulus came nearer, I noticed that the soldiers had up the three hundred yard sights. The bullets from the Zulus were now flying thickly, and several passed unpleasantly near to me, as, being on the top of the wagon, I was rather a good mark. The battle only lasted for a short time, but for that short time it was very hot. At last we beat them off and followed them for some distance, my men doing good work. I know I fired over thirty shots, and missed very few. I was much disappointed at the shooting of the soldiers. Their sole object seemed to be to get rid of ammunition or firing so many rounds per minute at anything—it didn't matter what —I calculated the loss on the side of the Zulus to be about seven hundred. Our loss was, comparatively, very small although many oxen and mules were killed. I had three of my men wounded. The battle was over early, and the rest of the day was spent in burying the dead and preparing for a forward march.

Whilst acceding to the request of Lord Chelmsford to accompany him, I had only agreed to go as far as the Inyezani River with him, my intention being, however, to go the whole way to Etshowe, but this I had not told him until now. and he seemed much pleased when I so announced my intention.

From the way that the Zulus scattered, I could see that it was a complete defeat for them, and that there was no danger of their again molesting us on the line of march, which turned out to be the case. We made an early start and reached the garrison at Etshowe late that evening, having travelled a distance of about fifteen miles. On the morning of the second day we again made a start on our return as we had accomplished our object, viz., the relief of the Etshowe garrison, and right glad was it to be free again. We returned to our laager at Ginginhlovu and then went on to Fort Pearson, on the Tugela, but we did not reach our destination that evening. We had to camp in a very nasty spot amongst bushes, but the moon being full it was a splendid night, so

that a man could be seen plainly at a distance of a hundred
yards. We turned in anyhow, as our blankets had miscarried.
Towards morning there was a false alarm, and I was roused
from a sound sleep by hearing firing and shouts. I seized
my rifle and jumped up, but what was my horror when I
recognised the voices of some of my unfortunate native scouts
calling out " Friend ! Friend !" which they had been taught
to respond to the challenge of the sentries. I called out,
" Good God ! they are shooting my men down !" and ran
out, calling out to the soldiers to stop firing. On passing the
line of fire I came upon one of my men lying dead in the
trench, with a bayonet wound in his chest. On examining
the lot I found ten more wounded, two of whom died the next
day. To account for this mishap, I must describe the mode
that had been adopted as regards the placing of the night
picquets that were stationed all round the encampment. My
men were stationed outside as fielders to the soldier picquets,
with orders that, on any alarm being given, they were to
retire in order on the soldiers, and each lot to retreat to the
enclosure. Well, it appears that an alarm had been given for
no cause whatever, and my men had retired and were coming
on with the soldiers, when, although it was known that there
was a picquet in that direction, they were taken to be Zulus.
The picquet, being of the 60th Rifles, wore dark uniforms.
The soldiers, without waiting to be certain, commenced firing.
The white picquet took the brunt of the firing off my men,
five of them being hit, and in trying to rush into the enclosure eleven of my men were bayonetted, three of whom died.

As soon as it was fairly day we moved on until we
reached the laager at Ginginhlovo, but the smell from the
dead being unpleasant, Lord Chelmsford did not stop there, but
we went on and formed camp about two miles further, on the
main road.

CHAPTER XV.

During the short time I was with Lord Chelmsford, the opinion that I formed of him was that he was a thorough gentleman and a good and brave soldier, but no General. Should this ever meet his eye, I hope he will forgive me, but my reason for forming this opinion was that I could see that his personal pluck led him to have no regard for the safety of his men. He would select any spot for a night encampment without studying the surroundings. Another of my reasons for my opinion was that he did not keep his men sufficiently together on the line of march, so much so that if the Zulus had been properly led they would have given us much trouble, and cut many a column up. Colonel Crealock—one of Lord Chelmsford's Staff, and brother to General Crealock (who was subsequently appointed to the command of the Lower Column) —came to me and said that he had been sent by Lord Chelmsford to beg me to join the Lower Column officially as Chief of the Intelligence Department, as he fully saw my worth, and felt assured I could be of much service to the Imperial Government, and of great assistance to General Crealock, who had just arrived in Natal, and was appointed to take command of the Lower, or Coast Column ; and that as he was a new man in the field, he would require some reliable assistance. I asked Colonel Crealock to give me time to think of the offer, which he did, and I saw I could be of service by inducing the Zulus to give up fighting, and per- haps might even persuade Cetywayo to come to terms, and thus put a stop to unnecessary bloodshed. Up to this time nothing had been said to me as to remuneration for my ser- vices, past and to come. Ultimately I decided to accept the offer, and so went to Lord Chelmsford and announced my intention of joining the Lower Column under General Crealock. He expressed his pleasure at my decision, and

said that, " as regards pay, you will receive the pay of a
Commandant, that is, thirty shillings a day, with rations for
yourself and two horses." This, he said, would commence
from the first day of my joining him at the Tugela, my time
being my own until I joined General Crealock.

I must not omit to mention one of those in command in
this column of the relief of the Etshowe garrison. I allude
to Commodore Richards of the Naval Brigade. I liked him
very much and we took to each other from the first night we
met, when we slept under a wagon together. He was a very
pleasant fellow. The Naval Brigade did good service. I
much preferred their style of going to work in action,
travelling, and things in general, to that adopted by the other
branch of the service.

As soon as we reached the Tugela Lord Chelmsford went
on to D'Urban to meet General Crealock and the Prince
Imperial of France, of whose arrival he had been apprised on
the night of our return. I followed a few days afterwards in
order to be introduced to General Crealock. On this occasion
I was fortunate enough to be introduced to many a good
fellow, amongst whom was Major Poole of the Artillery, who,
on the capture of Cetywayo, took charge of him, and was
with him at Capetown, until he (the Major) was ordered to
join the force sent against the Boers, and lost his life at
Laing's Neck, shortly after his arrival there. Whilst he was
in charge of Cetywayo, he wrote me the following letter,
enclosing one from Cetywayo, signed by himself, as taught
by Major Poole :—

                                    " Capetown, 29th October, 1880.
" DEAR SIR,—

    " I beg to enclose a letter from Cetywayo to you, which
I hope you will be able to answer—Cetywayo will look for a
reply. The letter is signed by Cetywayo himself. It was

written by me at his dictation. The photographs are sent by Cetywayo's direction, and I hope will reach you safely. Cetywayo will shortly be handed over to the Colonial Authorities, when he will lose sight of Longcast and myself. He is greatly attached to us, and I fear it will be a bitter parting.

"I hope that you are well and your country is settling down in a peaceful and prosperous state. I should be very glad to get a line from you to say that the letters and photographs reached you safely.

"If ever you should be sending this way—some Kafir medicine roots would please Cetywayo very much, also aloe leaves for his snuff which are difficult to obtain here.

"Believe me,

"Yours faithfully,

"(Signed)   W. RUSCOMBE POOLE."

The following is the enclosure from Cetywayo:—

"The Castle, Capetown, 29th October, 1880.

"*From Cetywayo to John Dunn, Zululand.*

"I send you greetings, and wish to tell you that I am in good health, and am well cared for, and that those who are looking after my wants are friendly and kind to me. They are the General [Clifford] the Colonel Commandant [Hussars] the Major [Poole] and Longcast. [The latter was the interpreter attached to Cetywayo's Staff.—ED.]

"I have suffered from rheumatism two or three times, but am quite well now. The doctors have been very kind and attentive to me, especially Drs. Cross and Bushe.

"All my people who are with me are well. They are Umkosana, Umtshingwayo, Umtigeza, Nozixobo, Xenisele, Puwase, Umpansi, and Uncebeza.

" Umsinda was sent away a week or two ago for miscon-
duct. He was insolent to me, and the Major punished him
and got him sent away.

" Why have you, John Dunn, forgotten me? If not, why
do you not send me news of my family ? I should be grate-
ful to you if you would do so. I hope you are kind to my
family, and enquire after them. I trust you do this in return
for many kindnesses you have received from me in years
past.

" I do not name the people I wish you to ask and report
to me about, as you know all my family well, and know who
I would like to hear of.

" Please send a message to Mahwanqna to say his daughter
Umpansi has been ill, but is now getting better—her chest
was wrong—an old complaint.

" I was *very* grieved to hear of the death of Gausi and
Umfusi. Pray send messages to their tribes to say I condole
with them.

" The General has given me photographs of Maduna and
Uziwetu, and the people who went with them to Natal. I
recognise all the faces. You must remember me to them,
and also to Dabulamanzi and Shingana.

" I send you three photographs of myself. They were
taken since my arrival in Capetown.

" I send this by Captain Baynton, who goes to Natal from
here to-day.

" CETYWAYO.'

[This letter was signed by Cetywayo's own hand, in
capitals that the Major had taught him to print.—ED.]

I answered the above letters but never heard of the receipt of the answers, owing, I think, to Major Poole's having left the Cape for Natal before he received them, and his subsequent death. About this time Bishop Colenso visited Cetywayo, after which, for the first time, I heard of Cetywayo's bitter tone against me.

On my being introduced to General Crealock by Commodore Richards, he said to me that from what he heard he had no doubt we would get on well together, that he did not know the exact date of his being able to take command at the front, but in the meantime I was to let him know of any information that I might obtain.

An advance post had now been established at the Inyezane River, called Fort Chelmsford. near the Ginginhlovu battle field, about twenty-five miles from Fort Pearson on the Tugela River. General Crealock was not detained long in D'Urban, and in due time arrived at Fort Pearson. The work of moving forward now commenced. Trains of transport wagons with provisions, and escort, were now being constantly despatched to Fort Chelmsford, and troops of cavalry and bodies of infantry sent forward until there was a considerable force there, and a large supply of provisions.

Chapter XVI.

My work now also commenced in earnest. Messengers from Cetywayo used to arrive at Fort Chelmsford, and were detained at that place, and I had to ride over there and receive these messages and send back the answers to them. On my arrival, on one occasion, at Fort Chelmsford, I was greatly amused to see a batch of these messengers being taken out for an airing by the soldiers, with nosebags covering their heads. This was a precaution taken to prevent spying. They certainly did look very ridiculous figures as they were led along thus blindfolded.

It took some considerable time before General Crealock could manage to get sufficient supplies to the front, owing to the slow transport, and as I was now in full swing of work, the delay was tedious to me, so I got permission to go in advance to Fort Chelmsford. Luckily, we had not to wait many days after my arrival there before General Crealock, with the main force, came up, and an advance was made towards Port Durnford. I was ordered to go with the advance column under Colonel Clark. I went on in front scouting with some of my men, with the object of trying to light on some Zulus and endeavouring to have some communication with them, and persuade them to come in and give themselves up, and by doing so enable me to send them round again and persuade many others of the folly of holding out. I felt convinced that as soon as it was known that I was with the troops many would listen to my voice and surrender, especially if it was known that all who did so would not be molested nor have their cattle taken from them. After a while I was fortunate enough to see a few stray Zulus, and on sending some of my men to them, two of them came up to us. I kept these two with us that night, and in the morning sent them with messages to different people of theirs. They were glad to be set free, saying that they would not have come in at all if they had not known my messengers personally, and therefore was certain that it was I who sent for them. I was now leading the column a short cut in the direction of Port Durnford, so after two days' march we came to the Umlalazi River, and as, owing to the heavy rains, it was too deep to ford, a bridge of pontoons had to be made. This took two days, and in the meantime the whole force came up. I rode over with a few of my men, and again espied a few Zulus sitting on a hill. I again sent a man to call them, and one came to me, and I at once sent him off to a man named Guzana, whom I knew well, telling him to come to me the next day with his people. On my return I informed General Crealock of what I had done, and he arranged with me to go next day and meet Guzana. The next day I got a message from the latter to say that he sent the bearer first to ascertain whether it was really my own self who wanted to see him, and if it was, the man was to say that he would meet me at a spot a few miles off, which I was to name, as he was afraid to come in among the soldiers.

Accordingly, about two o'clock we went over and met him, with about six men, and we, including the General and myself, only numbered five. After a little talk, the General told him the terms of submission, and told him to bring all his family in the next day. This he promised to do, and did, coming in with about a hundred and fifty men, women, and children. We had a nice little family now on our hands, but as food was plentiful they were not much trouble. I now had plenty of available men to carry on communication with, and whom I could now send to the different head men I knew and advise them to come in.

We now advanced to Port Durnford. But before proceeding further, I must not omit to mention an unfortunate accident that happened to the General. The day after Guzana came in we were riding round in the direction of Guzana's kraals, when we espied a cow running towards us. The General called out, " The first man that reaches her can claim her," and he started off. I was in advance, and was reining-in my horse to give the General the lead, which, fortunately for me, he took. As soon as he got up to the cow she charged him, and before he had time to get out of her

way, she struck his horse with her horn between his hind
legs, ripping out his entrails. I then shot the cow ; but the
General lost a good horse, as it died shortly afterwards. The
General was a very good shot with the rifle. One day we
were riding along, and saw a Paauw (Bustard). I always
used to carry my rifle, and I handed it to the General to have
a shot at the bird, which was a couple of hundred yards away.
He took aim, and dropped it.

When we got to Port Durnford we found a vessel
waiting for us there, and we had not been there many days
before the effects of the peaceful messages to the Natives
became apparent. Hardly a day passed without someone
coming in with his family, and in a short time the country
was swarming with people who had surrendered, and brought
all their cattle with them. I received instructions to select
all the cattle that had belonged to Cetywayo, and to return
the remainder to their owners. About this time we received
the news of Sir Garnet Wolseley's landing at Natal. He had
come to supercede both Lord Chelmsford and General Crealock, and, at a certain day, was to be at Port Durnford.
That day having arrived, he appeared, and signalled from his
ship that he wished to see me as soon as he had landed, and I
received orders to be down on the beach in waiting, but
owing to the weather turning out to be too rough, he could
not land, and had to return to Natal and come by land.
Before he arrived at our camp, however, we received the news
that Lord Chelmsford had fought a battle at Ulundi, and, that
the Zulus had, even by their own account, been completely
defeated. People from all over the country now began to
come in to where they heard I was, and that from distances
of sixty and seventy miles. On Sir Garnet Wolseley's
arrival, and his taking over the command, General Crealock
gave him a paper, of which the following is a copy, which he
gave me :—

" Head Quarters, First Division,

" Umlazi Plains, 7th July, 1879.

"The Military Secretary,

" His Excellency General Sir

" GARNET WOSELEY, K.C.B.

" SIR,—On the occasion of handing over the political
direction of the affairs of Zululand, connected with this
column, which I have hitherto conducted under orders from
Lord Chelmsford and Sir Bartle Frere, I beg to be allowed to
call the attention of His Excellency General Sir Garnet
Wolseley to the invaluable services performed by Mr. John
Dunn, attached to me as Political and Intelligence Officer by
Lord Chelmsford.

" It is impossible for me exaggerate the useful information obtained by this officer, not only for me, but also for
Lord Chelmsford. His great knowledge of this country and
of its people, his long residence in it, and the perfect confidence evidently reposed in him by all classes of Zulus, have
not only been most useful to me from a military point of
view, but have also undoubtedly tended more than anything
else to bring about the satisfactory condition of things which
I have already had occasion to report to His Excellency, viz.,
the submission of many influential Chiefs of this District,
with their families and followers, and their cattle.

" I have found his local information regarding roads,
rivers, and natural obstacles, remarkably accurate, and of the
greatest service.

" Mr. Dunn was, I am aware, very averse to taking
service of the nature he is now performing, but at the earnest
request of Lord Chelmsford, who had learnt to value him, as
I have, he consented to accompany me in his present position.

H

"I have found him perfectly reliable and perfectly trust-
worthy, and silence and discretion itself, and I cannot too
strongly recommend him to the favour of His Excellency.

"I have the honour to be,

"Sir,

"Your most obedient Servant,

"(Signed)   H. HOPE CREALOCK,

"Major-General,

"C.I.D.

A day or two afterwards, Sir Garnet held a meeting of all
the chiefs who had surrendered, and after his telling them the
condition of surrender, he asked them if they had anything to
say.   Undhlandaga, one of the principal headmen, acted as
spokesman, and said, " Our word is but one—we wish no more
for a black King—we wish for a white one, and the white
one we mean is that one (pointing to me) John Dunn. He
knows us, and knows our ways, and we know him and like
him." The rest of the men then said " our voice is one, we
say the same."   Dr. Russell, the correspondent of the London
Times, who was present, turning to me, said, " Well, Dunn,
that is a great compliment, and one that you might well be
proud of."   After the meeting was over, Sir Garnet took me
to his tent, and on thanking me for my services, said that he
understood that I held a tract of country with a tribe under
me as an independent Chief, and asked me if I should like
this tract extended. I said, yes, I should be glad of it, and
after a conversation as to the future settlement, and examining a map, we separated. Preparations for breaking up now
began ; we, that is the part of the column that was to proceed
with Sir Garnet to the Ulundi (for the purpose of getting
Cetywayo to surrender or capture him) and General Crealock
and his staff. I had got on well with the General who was a
a very pleasant gentleman, and many a fat fowl had I helped
to demolish at his table.

The opinion that I formed of this General was that he was a good commanding officer, looking well after his commissariat, and sick in the Hospital, but if ever he should read this, he must excuse me for saying that if fighting had occurred he would not have shone as a General. But I might be wrong.

CHAPTER XVII.

I was now under command of my third General, Sir Garnet Wolseley, who was accompanied by his brilliant staff. Our part of the column, under Colonel Clark, now moved on to the Umhlatuzi River, from which encampment it was the intention of Sir Garnet to go and meet Lord Chelmsford, who was on his way homewards from Ulundi, and on his (Sir Garnet's) return, start back for Natal and join a column that was to be formed in an up-country division of that column, and proceed with it and meet us near Ulundi. Large numbers of people and cattle continued to come in daily, and messages also from Cetywayo, but without any tone of submission. From here I sent three of my own men to him trying to persuade him to come in himself and surrender, offering, if he would do so, to go and meet him. On Sir Garnet's return from meeting Lord Chelmsford, I had some misunderstanding with a Mr. Fynney who was acting as an interpreter to Sir Garnet. As he was meddling in my business, which very much annoyed me, I went to Sir Garnet and begged him to allow me to resign, stating my reason. This request of mine Sir Garnet would not listen to, saying, " No, Dunn, I think you will find it to your advantage to remain with me until this business is over. Mr. Fynney returns from here with me." On these conditions I consented to remain, and proceeded with Colonel Clark ; Sir Garnet and his

H2

party returning to Natal. Nothing of any note happened
on the way to Ulundi. One night as I was returning to my
wagon, having dined with Colonel Clark, I was much amused
on hearing a conversation between some young soldiers going
to relieve guard, and who were walking in front of me. It
was a very cold wet night, and one of them was saying something that I could not catch. One of his companions said to
him, however, "There is not a bit of use in your grumbling
my fine fellow, when a man once enlists to be a soldier not
even his blessed tongue is his own ; even every hair of your
head is all fixed bayonets." I thought this was very good as
it proved how much a good soldier thought himself a mere
machine. Sir Garnet overtook us at the foot of the Intonjanini—the site of Cetywayo's late installation by Sir Theo.
Shepstone. The General was accompanied by Mr. J.
Shepstone, the Acting Secretary for Native Affairs. I was
glad to see this as it did away with with my friend Mr.
Fynney. This was, I think, the coldest night I ever felt. I
dined with Sir Garnet that night, and I know I was very glad
to reach my wagon and get between the blankets. On the
line of march I had the advantage of many in having my
own wagon and provisions with me, as also plenty of liquor
stuff, so as not to be dependant upon rations. I was fortunate
enough to give many a hungry fellow a good feed and drink.

On the morning after this cold night, one hundred and
seven oxen were found dead and tied to the yokes—a great
loss. My own team I had directed my driver to allow to run
loose to take their chance, which was fortunate, for they
found a sheltered nook in a ravine, and were, consequently,
all right. From this place we went on, leaving the column
to follow, as Sir Garnet had made up his mind to camp on
the site of the Ulundi Kraal. On arriving there the time
was passed in looking for curios. Amongst those found was

a portrait of the Queen, which was dug up by some of Sir
Garnet's Staff. It had suffered much by its burial, but was
nevertheless a trophy. This picture, I well recollected, used
to hang in Cetywayo's European cottage which he had had
built inside the kraal. Often when I had been sitting with
him, before he had been spoilt by the faction I have spoken
of, he, on looking at the picture, had said, "There is my
mother—I would be glad to see her." He little thought
then how soon his wish was to be fulfilled in a way he never
dreamed of. We only spent one night on the site of the
Ulundi Kraal, and the next day Sir Garnet moved on about
three miles further.

The messengers that I had sent to Cetywayo had, in the
meantime, returned without having been able to see him, his
place of hiding being kept secret. The day we arrived here
a Hollander of the name of Vijn, who had been with Cetywayo during the whole time of the war, came with a message
from the latter to Sir Garnet, and was sent back with an
answer. As Cetywayo now refused to give himself up,
parties were organised to search for and capture him. After
considerable trouble he was at length taken. Thus ended his
reign for a time, and thus was the Zulu power broken.

A day was now fixed for a meeting of all the headmen
of the country, and the appointment of Chiefs, as Sir Garnet
had decided to cut the country up into thirteen different in-
dependencies. He sent his Private Secretary with a copy of
the conditions under which the Chiefs were to be appointed,
asking me if I would accept a Chieftainship. After reading
the conditions over *I assented, on condition that Cetywayo
should never hold any position in the country again.* To this
Sir Garnet gave his word, and on this condition I accepted
the Chieftainship.

Such was the rise and fall of Cetywayo, and the end of an unjust war —not to Cetywayo, but to the Zulu nation. It was a fine race, and if it had only been properly handled and treated as an independent power, it would have been a staunch ally of England. The prime cause of the ruin of the Zulu nation was the tone of authority assumed towards the Zulu Kings by those wielding the Government of Natal—a tone presumed on by the native messengers sent by that Government, and a tone which rankled in the breast of the last King until it broke out into expressions of disgust towards the Government, which, being spoken out publicly, were taken up by the people, and eventually led to a bad feeling towards the whites.

I say the war was unjust, because I think that there was no valid reason for it, although, as long as the Natal Government held their dictatorial tone, it would have come sooner or later. The so-called settlement of Zululand was the maddest piece of policy ever heard of, as the Zulu people, after their defeat, naturally looked upon themselves as subjects of the Government, and then they would willingly have allowed themselves to be moulded into any shape. The country ought to have been annexed and brought under British rule at first, without sending Cetywayo away.

The Settlement as made by Sir Garnet Wolseley, having no alternative, would have worked well for some years, if the Resident had been vested with greater authority, and a small force had been at his command to carry out his orders. But seeing that he had not been vested by that authority, he should have been content with his nominal position, and merely advised the Chiefs, instead of doing what he did. If any trivial complaint against an appointed Chief was brought to him, he would go through the form of taking down the complaint in writing, which course naturally gave rise to the idea that any commoner could bring a complaint against a Chief, and that the Chiefs were assuming an authority they did not possess. I spoke to the Resident shortly after his appointment, to the above effect, but I suppose he had his instructions. The Settlement would have worked well, had it not been only an experiment, for some time. If it had not been for this, and the outside agitation, I say things would have gone better. But the Resident had no power to check this outside agitation. Another great cause of failure has lain in the fact of the Resident assuming a tone of authority he did not possess, and yet being afraid of acting on his own responsibility in any case — when he saw that by so doing he could do good—combined with the fear of criticism and interference of the late Bishop Colenso.

The War against the Zulus was an unjust one, but the restoration of Cetywayo to power, after having taken him away from his people and dividing them into sections, has proved itself a much greater act of injustice, as witness the great loss of life that has taken place in the short time that has passed since his return. A calamity that, I predicted in letters to my friends.

CHAPTER XVIII.

The day of the great meeting at length arrived, and there was a large assembly. I was the first Chief who was formally appointed, and I signed the following document, all the other Chiefs doing the same as regards their respective appointments. The following is a copy of my deed of Chieftainship :—

" I recognise the victory of the British arms over the
Zulu nation and the full right and title of Her
Majesty Queen Victoria, Queen of England and
Empress of India, to deal as she may think fit with
the Zulu Chiefs and people, and with the Zulu
Country, and I agree, and I hereby signify my
agreement to accept from General Sir Garnet
Joseph Wolseley, G.C.M.G., K.C.B., as the Repre-
sentative of Her Majesty Queen Victoria, the
Chieftainship of a territory of Zululand to be known
hereafter as

JOHN DUNN'S TERRITORY,

subject to the following terms, conditions, and
limitations :—

" Terms, conditions, and limitations laid down by
General Sir Garnet Joseph Wolseley, G.C.M.G.,
K.C.B., and assented to by me, JOHN DUNN, Chief,
as the terms, conditions, and limitations, subject to
which I agree to accept the Chieftainship of the
aforesaid territory :—

" 1. I will observe and respect whatever boundaries shall
be assigned to my territory by the British Government, through the Resident of the Division in
which my territory is situated.

" 2. I will not permit the existence of the Zulu Military
System, or the existence of any military system or
organisation whatever within my territory, and I
will proclaim and make it a rule that all men shall
be allowed to marry when they choose, and as they
choose, according to the good and ancient customs
of my people, known and followed in the days pre-
ceding the establishment by Tshaka of the system

known as the military system, and I will allow and encourage all men living within my territory to go and come freely for peaceful purposes, and to work in Natal and the Transvaal or elsewhere for themselves or for hire.

" 3. I will not import or allow to be imported into my territory by any person upon any pretence or for any object whatsoeve, any arms or ammunition, from any part whatsoever, any goods or merchandize, by the sea coast of Zululand, without the express sanction of the Resident of the Division in which my territory is situated, and I will not encourage, or promote, or take part in, or countenance in any way whatsoever the importation into any other part of Zululand of arms or ammunition, from any part whatsoever, or of goods and merchandise by the sea coast of Zululand, without such sanction ; and I will confiscate and hand over to the Natal Government all arms, ammunition, and goods and merchandize so imported into my territory ; and I will punish by fine or other sufficient punishment any person guilty of or concerned in such unsanctioned importation, and any person found possessing arms or ammunition, or goods or merchandize, knowingly obtained thereby.

" 4. I will not allow the life of any of my people to be taken for any cause, except after sentence passed in a council of the chief men of my territory, and after fair and impartial trial in my presence, and after the hearing of witnesses ; and I will not tolerate the employment of witch doctors, or the practise known as " smelling out " or any practis of witchcraft.

" 5. The surrender of all persons, fugitives in my territory from justice, when demanded by the Government of any British Colony, territory, or province,
in the interests of justice, shall be readily and
promptly made to such Government, and the escape
into my territory of persons accused or convicted of
offences against British laws, shall be prevented by
all possible means, and every exertion shall be used
to seacrh for and deliver up such persons to British
authority.

" 6. I will not make war upon any Chief or Chiefs, or
people without the sanction of the British Government, and in any unsettled dispute with any Chief
or people, I will appeal to the arbitration of the
British Government through the Resident 'of the
Division in which my territory is situated

" 7. The succession to the Chieftainship of my territory
shall be according to the ancient laws and customs
of my people, and the nomination of each successor
shall be subject to the approval of the British
Government.

" 8. I will not sell or in any way alienate, or permit, or
countenance any sale or alienation of any part of
the land in my territory.

" 9. I will permit all people now residing within my
territory to there remain upon the condition that
they recognise my authority as Chief, and any person not wishing to recognise my authority as Chief,
and desirous to quit my territory, I will permit to
quit it, and to pass unmolested elsewhere.

" 10. In all cases of dispute in which British subjects
are involved I will appeal to and abide by the

decision of the British Resident of the Division in which my territory is situated, and in all cases where accusations of offences or crimes committed in my territory, are brought against British subjects or against my people in relation to British subject, I will hold no trial, and pass no sentence, but with the approval of such British Resident.

" 11. In all matters not included within these terms, conditions, and limitations, and for all cases unprovided for herein, and in all cases where there may be doubt and uncertainty as to the laws, rules, or stipulations, applicable to matters to be dealt with, I will govern, order, and decide in accordance with the ancient laws and usage of my people.

" These terms, conditions, and limitations, I engage, and solemnly pledge my faith to abide by and respect in letter and in spirit, without qualification or reserve.

" Signed at Ulundi on this 1st day of September, 1879.

"(Signed)   J. R. DUNN,

"(Signed)   G. J. WOLSELEY,

" General Commanding Forces in South Africa, and H.M. High Commmissioner for South Africa."

The next morning after the Settlement, preparations were made for a break-up, Sir Garnet to start off for the subjugation of Sekukuku (commonly and erroneously spelt Sekukuni), and I to return with Colonel Clarke's Column to take possession of my territory.

Let self-considered wiser heads than mine say what they like, I am confident that if my services had been more

utilised, even after the restoration of Cetywayo, I could
greatly have assisted in bringing about a more peaceful
settlement of affairs in this country, from my actual knowledge of the feelings of the people. But no, I was set up by
a certain faction, *to suit their end*, as a rival to Cetywayo,
hence the consequences.

The opinion that I formed of Sir Garnet was that he
was a good General, a thorough soldier, and, in fact, a man
fit for any emergency. I had got on very well with him and
liked him, and in pointing out different important situations
to him we had many a pleasant ride together.

I have now recorded the opinions I have formed con-
cerning the three Generals under whom I served in my
capacity as head of the Native Intelligence Department.
Shortly after getting settled in my territory I received a most
amusing number of letters from all parts of the world, some
containing applications for situations—others for pecuuiary
assistance—others from people (of the same name as myself)
claiming relationship with me as daughters, sons, nephews,
nieces, &c., but the most amusing one I got was from a
woman claiming to be my wife. She said I had deserted her
thirty-six years ago in Ireland. I need hardly say that I did
not know one of the writers ; in fact, never heard of them
before. For the amusement of my readers I give a few of
them, though, of course, leaving out the names of the writers
Some other letters I received from people begging me to
secure their safety when Cetywayo was on the eve of attack-
ing the Transvaal Boers.

But before inserting the letters above alluded to, which,
with a few other matters, will form an Appendix to this work,
I beg to insert a copy of the following letter from the present
Lord Wolseley to the Earl of Derby :—

"Horse Guards, War Office,

"31st January, 1883.

"The Right Hon. The EARL OF DERBY,

&c.,   &c.,

"Colonial Office.

"MY LORD,—I have the honour to forward you the enclosed letter and paper from Mr. John Dunn, whom I understand has lately been deprived of his position as Chief in Zululand by order of Her Majesty's Government.

"From the terms of his letter I presume he wishes me to lay it before you.

"I feel bound to state that Mr. Dunn would not have accepted the position of Chief had I not, as Her Majesty's High Commissioner, given him a promise in the name of the Government of England that under no circumstances should Cetywayo be ever allowed to return to Zululand—a promise approved of by the Government of the day, as your Lordship will learn from a perusal of the correspondence that took place between me and the Colonial Office in 1879–80, on the subject of the Settlement of Zululand.

"Mr. Dunn did not ask to be made a Chief—he was made so because it was believed that his acceptance of that position would further the South African policy of Her Majesty's Government at the time, and would conduce to the benefit of Natal, as well as those over whom he was placed as ruler.

"I have the honour to be,

"My Lord,

"Your Lordship's most obedient Servant,

"(Signed)   WOLSELEY."

APPENDIX.

" [CONFIDENTIAL.]

" Office of Secretary for Native Affairs,
" Natal, 3rd April, 1876.

" SIR,—I am directed by the Lieutenant-Governor of Natal to acknowledge the receipt of your letter of the 13th ultimo, which was duly delivered by the Zulu messengers.

" I enclose for your information, copy of His Excellency's reply to the message brought by them, which reply has, of course, been delivered to the messengers verbally.

" The Lieutenant-Governor trusts that you will impress upon Cetywayo the importance of abstaining from and preventing any act of aggressiveness on the part of his people.

" You will understand that His Excellency does not attribute to Cetywayo any such disposition, on the contrary, he is fully sensible that Cetywayo has always paid much attention to the wishes of this Government, so frequently represented to him, with regard to his relations with the Government of the Transvaal, and His Excellency has not failed to bring this circumstance under the due notice of Her Majesty's Government.

" You are probably aware that Her Majesty's Government have proposed that a Conference of Represetatives from the different Governments and States in South Africa should be held in London this year, at which various questions of difference may be discussed and settled, and it would be unfortunate, if at such a meeting, any aggressive act on the part of the Zulu people could be truly averred against them.

"This Government will be represented by myself, and possibly by others as well, at that Conference.

"Should Cetywayo desire to make any further statement on the subject of his difference with the Transvaal Government, the Lieutenant-Governor will be prepared to forward it to the Secretary of State.

"This Government has urged upon the Government of the Transvaal, as it has upon Cetywayo, the great importance of moderation and of preserving the peace between the two countries, and he trusts that should a Conference be held, a means may be found of bringing to a satisfactory and equitable termination this long-vexed question.

"I have the honour to be,
"Sir,
"Your obedient Servant,

"T. Shepstone,
"Secretary for Native Affairs.

"J. Dunn, Esq.,
"Zulu Country."

Written by me (John Dunn) shortly after the 3rd of April, 1876, to Sir Theophilus Shepstone, at the request of Cetywayo:—

"STATEMENT OF CETYWAYO AND HIS INDUNAS.

"We ignore any right or claim for land by the Dutch Boers on the Zulu Nation, as Tshaka, the founder of the Zulu tribe, claimed all the land from under the Drakensberg Moun-

tains to the sea, by right of conquest. We first formed
relationship to the English by saving the lives of seven
Englishmen who were wrecked at the mouth of the Umfolozi
river, or St. Lucia Bay, and we sent them to the present Port
of D'Urban. Shortly afterwards we sent Sotobe, by sea, to
the Cape, to form a firmer alliance with the English. Before
his return Tshaka was slain. Tshaka was accompanied on
three different expeditions by the few Englishmen that were
in Natal, and he always said the English were the only
relatives the Zulus had. After Tshaka's death, his successor
Dingaan was also accompanied, in some expeditions, by the
English, and the first intimation they—the Zulus—had of the
Boers was when Dingaan went out on an expedition to
Umzilikazi, when the Boers came and claimed some cattle
which the Zulus had taken from Umzilikazi (who was a
revolted Zulu Chieftain), saying that these cattle had been
taken from them, the Boers, in a fight. Our second experience of them was when, on the part of Dingaan, they
retook some cattle which Sikomyela had stolen from the
former. Afterwards the massacre of them at Dingaan's
Kraal occurred, and then we had war with them, when Panda
(Cetywayo's father) mistaking, in his ignorance, the Boers
for Englishmen, formed a treaty with them, and turned
against his brother Dingaan, and, with the Boers, fought
against him, although at the fight Panda and his men were
not present. It was mere empty form saying Panda was
made King by the Boers, although the Boers, stating that
such was the case, made a heavy claim of cattle and children
on the nation. If the Dutch Boers had been, as they assert,
on a friendly footing with the late King Panda, why was it
that when the latter sent out an army against the Amaswazi,
the Boers refused to give up cattle that ran to them from the
Swazi?

" On the English defeating the Dutch Boers (or Emigrant
Farmers of the Cape Colony) a party of Boers came and
presented Panda with a h undred head of cattle, and asked for
some land in the upper co untry, across the Buffalo River,
where Langalibalele then li ved (Bekezulu), saying that they
wished to act as a buffer between the English and Zulus, to
which Panda agreed. Cetywayo repudiates any further
claim by the Boers on the Zulu country, as, on a pressing
occasion, when the late King Panda was alive, Cetywayo
went with a lot of his followers after some brothers of his
who had fled to the Boers, but who were given up to him.
On this occasion the Boers tried to get him to give them
some land, which he refused to do. The Boers then made
him a present of some cattle without any stipulation what--
ever. On Cetywayo afterwards hearing that the Boers said'
they had given these cattle for land, he at once returned such
cattle. After the lapse of some time, it came to his knowledge that his father Panda (properly Um'Pande) had received
some cattle and sheep from the Dutch, and hearing that, in
consequence, the Boers again laid claim to land, he advised:
the Indunas to return the cattle. On several occasions have
the Boers tried by representations to get documents signed.
by the late King Panda and Cetywayo for grants of land, but
have always been refused. On a pretext of a right to land,
the Boers have constantly kept the Zulu border in an unsettled state by harbouring people from the Zulu country who
have taken the King's cattle away with them, which the
Boers, in their turn, deprive them of and keep them. Cetywayo and his Indunas deny any claim that the Boers have
for land in the Zulu country, as on one occasion when the
question was again raised, the Indunas had two hundred head
of cattle collected and sent back to the Boers, who would not
receive them, declaring that Panda had given them the land,

I

but the latter King, on being questioned by the Indunas, denied that he had given away land. Shortly after this it was reported by the people on the borders that the Boers were putting up a line of beacons, cutting off a large portion of the Zulu country. On this becoming known, some of the Chiefs living in the neighbourhood ordered a lot of young men to pull up these beacons, which was done. Since this occurred, a Boer came with some Kafirs and destroyed a kraal, and on some people trying to prevent him, he fired at them and wounded a young Zulu. On another occasion some Boers came and requested Panda to place one of his headmen near them, naming a spot, which the King consented to do, and on Zingwayo being sent, and upon his building a kraal, another party of Boers came and pulled it down. Upon another occasion a man was shot by a Boer for refusing to assist in skinning a cow. No notice was taken of this by the Boers. We state these facts to show that no aggressive acts have been committed by the Zulus. All these facts were duly reported to the British Government, and when Mr. Shepstone came to this country to crown Cetywayo, the facts were again reported, and he was begged to try and settle the question, so as to prevent a war, which he promised to do, also to consult with the Governor of Natal about the matter, and a whiteman named Taylor was sent with some of the Indunas to see about the disputed boundary, and Mr. Shepstone was to have let Cetywayo know what steps would be taken.

"Since the above, the Boers have, on several occasions and on several pretexts, taken cattle, to the number of upwards of thirty, and have often beaten men, women, and children, and they lately took a Zulu named Manyonyob a prisoner, alleging for excuse that he had killed one of his own people.

"We, as a nation, now perceive that the Boers want to have trouble with us, because, the English—they openly say, are our protectors, aud not the Boers.

" Another great question with us is about the Amaswazi, who were formerly our people, as Sobuza, their great original chief was one of Tshaka's people, to whom he gave a lot of cattle, but the Amaswasi are now claimed by the Boers. This is also a question Cetywayo and his Indunas earnestly beg His Excellency will make enquiry into and ascertain on what grounds the Boers are acting.

" The Amaswazi need punishment from us—the cattle that they have were originally the property of the Zulus.

" The thirty three head of cattle that the Boers have taken—as stated before—we beg the Governor will write to the Boers about, and have them returned, as they are, at present, the cause of trouble, as, if not returned, their owner is likely to help himself out of the cattle of the Boers.

" Not long ago another man of ours was taken prisoner by the Boers for allowing some people who had returned in allegiance to the Zulu country to stay at his kraal.

" Cetywayo earnestly begs that His Excellency the Lieutenant Governor will see him righted in this land question as it belongs to the Zulu nation by right of conquest, and he doees not wish to go to war about it.

The above was written in answer to Sir Theo. Shepstone's letter of April 3rd, 1876, and was supposed to have been taken home by him to lay before the Secretary of State, but nothing more was heard of it until the return of Sir Theo. from England, when his change in favour of the Boers became apparent at the Blood River Meeting. It was in allusion to this change of front that Bishop Colense said that Sir Theo. was no friend of Cetywayo's.

I 2

TRANSLATION.

[No. 913].

" Government Office, South African Republic,

"Pretoria, 26th April, 1876.

" *Thomas Francois Burgers, President of the South African
    Republic, to Ketywayo, Supreme Chief and King of the
    Zulus.*

" GOOD FRIEND,—

" I am glad to be able to inform you that I have returned
in good health after a long illness and absence to Europe.
And I will be glad to ascertain that it goes well with you and
that you are well and in good health.

" I rejoice to see that during my absence peace has been
maintained between the Republic and Zululand, although I
much regret that many disturbances have taken place upon
the border. Such disturbances and quarrels are not only
very detrimental to the border people of both countries themselves, but are very dangerous to the peace that is so very
desirable to the population of both countries.

" I am, as ever, desirous to live in peace and friendship
with my neighbours and in particular with Ketywayo and his
people.

" This peace and friendship cannot, however, continue to
exist long unless the dispute about the boundary line be
settled. It is for that reason that I now propose to you to let
me know whether you are willing to have yourself represented
by plenipotentiaries of a meeting to be held in the course of
a couple of months, somewhere along the Blood River in
order to negotiate in a friendly manner about the boundary
question, and to make a final end of quarrel and variances.

" The boundary line could then be permanently beaconed off and be surveyed so that no fear can remain of a recurrence of disturbances about boundary questions.

" I believe that by indulgence on both sides it will be possible to arrive at a friendly arrangement of the matter.

" Trusting that you, filled with the same desire as myself to arrange all in peace, will let me know as soon as possible whether Monday the 3rd of July next will be a suitable day for the meeting.

" I am, your Friend,

" (Signed)   THOS. BURGERS,

" State President of the South
African Republic.

" By order,

"(Signed)   SWART,

" State Secretary.

" A true translation,
" (Signed)   G. M. RUDOLPH,

" Landdrost."

" Chirley Valley, Utrecht,
" 20th February, 1877.

" J. DUNN, Esq.,

" MY DEAR SIR,— I have been requested by several British and German subjects to communicate to you for the King Cetywayo that, in the event of war between the Boers of this Republic and the Zulus, no British or German subjects will take part on either side, but remain neutral.

"They beg to request that their neutrality may be respected and not be liable to molestation in person or property.

"To avoid any mistake or misunderstanding in the event of a war, the subjects of both nations would rally under their respective national flags on some spot on the Pongola over the disputed line.

"The Boer Government are not allowed to commandeer British subjects resident in the Transvaal. There are nearly fifty European families residing about the Pongola valley.

"Will you please consult Cetywayo on the subject, and send an early reply.

"There is no dependence on the Boers accepting the Federation under the British Flag. They are getting quite bounceable since Secocoeni has offered to make peace.

"With kind regards,

'Yours truly,

"(Signed)   E. F. RATHBONE.

"P.S.—Any suggestion of your own as to how we ought to act under the circumstances would be thankfully received. Up to the present time the English and Germans have not gone into the Boer laager, always believing that they would not be interfered with by the Zulus if they were known not to be Boers.

"If Federation is not carried, and Paul Kruger is elected President, there will be war for a certainty."

It has been stated that the main cause of the Home Government having changed their views of Lord Wolseley's settlement of Zululand and restoring Cetywayo was on account of the disagreement amongst the appointed Chiefs, I can with confidence say this was not the case, as there was hardly a single instance of disagreement amongst any of the appointed Chiefs.

This the Resident Commissioner must know to be the case.

The only cases of disturbances were caused by rebellion of subjects against their Chiefs, incited by emissaries of the late Bishop Colenso and others, which could have been easily checked if the Resident Commissioner could have given the slightest countenance to such restraint, as for instance, when I took, to a certain degree, responsibility on myself and quelled an usurper named Sitimela, who represented himself as coming from Mr. J. Shepstone and Mr. Fynney to claim the Umtetwa Chieftainship.

"Transvaal Republic, May, 1876.

" *Mr. John Dunn,*

" DEAR SIR,—We Englishmen generally sympathise with the Zulus, believing that the Dutch have greatly wronged them by taking their land from them, but as we are only a few compared with them, the latter, who are numerous, we cannot help ourselves, but have to contribute largely in money towards their expenses ; as well as in almost every case to give personal assistance also, or get our property confiscated, imprisoned, or probably shot, if siding with the Zulus or Maccatees against this Government, yet all the time feeling how unjustly they are acting towards the natives, and I firmly believe nearly all the English who have to join the Boers in fighting against them if they knew they could depend upon the Zulus after the first meeting and brush, would consider it no crime or disgrace, but a righteous act to go over to the Zulus.

" This Transvaal Government is commandeering strongly to go against Siccokuni, who is also believed by Englishmen to have just cause to rebel against the Boers.

" I however hope and trust that whenever Siccokuni or the Zulus meet the Boer commando, if they gain any advantages over it, they will not forget to spare women and children for if they do this, they will receive the good wishes and probably future services and assistance not only from the English people, but the English Government also, for the latter sooner or later will have to take upon themselves the Government of this Republic and part of South Africa.

" I remain,

" Yours faithfully,

"THE MAN WHO USED TO RIDE YOUR
WHITE PACK OX WHEN A BOY."

" District Newcastle, January 9th, 1876.

"*Mr. John Dunn,*

" DEAR SIR,—I did not wish to stop longer in the Transvaal and so am here. I wish to advise you to look out for squalls, for all the fighting men are ordered to the Zulu border, for although 3 men where sent down from the Government to see Ketchwayo and say the boers did not want to fight, which is true if they can get the country without, but you must not trust them for they lie like thieves, and will fight when they have done for poor Sicikon and his people, and find themselves strong enough for destroying the Zulus, therefore now or never is your time to tumble down all beacons and houses upon Zulu territory, and hunt all rogues out of the Country, but be sure you do not kill or molest women and children, although belonging to your enemies, as it would get you a bad name from Englishmen and the Government as well as other Governments, and perhaps induce other Governments to assist against the Zulus. I wish I was Commander-in-Chief for one month instead of you, and I would let all rogues and thieves know what Chalka's people could do. Please destroy this when read, and if you want to hear from me again you can write to me here at Newcastle. You will know what to call me when you know I am Comearpy's old master, also tell me who I can enclose my letters to you at Tugela so they don't fall into the wrong persons hands."

[This letter is written in the same handwriting as that of the man who subsequently signs himself as the man who rode "The White Pack Ox."—ED].

" Office of the Zulu Border Agent,
" Utrecht, March 21, 1876.

" SIR,—In acknowledging your letter of the 21st inst., written, as you say, at the request of the Zulu King, I am glad to have the opportunity of explaining to Cetywayo that the reports brought to him are one-sided, and incorrect in many points. I understand this from your letter.

" It is not true that a party of some white men and some Kafirs have been going from kraal to kraal seizing cattle and beating and ill-treating his subjects.

" I have explained all to Sijulana, Umbemba, and Umvoko, how and what was done. So far as I know fifteen cattle were taken as a fine from Bukwini and other kraals. The Field-cornet sent native people to two or three kraals on occupied farms giving notice to pay Government taxes. The police were attacked, and returned to the Fieldcornet. A couple of days afterwards the Fieldcornet went with four or five men and some police. The people of the kraal went for their sticks and arms, and the Fieldcornet punished them there and then and fined them. This was at Bukwini's kraal. It went similarly at Umpungana's and Dinzela's kraal.

"Please tell the Chief that I have stopped this and the tax at once. I have given all my words to his man Sijulana, having reference to the whole matter.

"I will bring his complaint about his cattle before His Honour the President, who will be back in Pretoria from Europe on the 10th April next. I am going there myself to explain everything by word of mouth, and Cetywayo shall have his answer without delay.

"Sijulana will tell the Chief how the people came in large armed commandos on the 9th and 10th to the houses of the farmers, and how they took away things from the homesteads and destroyed other things. Why is this so? I cannot think that Cetywayo wants to make war with us. We don't want war with him. If we have a difference, why can't we settle it peaceably, Why did he not complain to me (if he felt wronged by what the Fieldcornets did). He knows that I always listen to what he has to say, and try to help him.

"I am glad, dear Dunn, that you are at the Chief's kraal. You can now interpret this letter to him properly.

"I am, Sir,

"Yours truly,

"(Signed)   G. M. RUDOLPH,

"Zulu Border Agent.

"P.S.—Please desire the Chief to order his people on the border to be quiet also."

[COPY.]

"Reply of the Lieutenant-Governor of Natal to the Message from Cetywayo, King of the Zulus, by Matyana, Ugeoza and Unyame, delivered at Pietermaritzburg on the 31st March, 1876.

"The Lieutenant-Governor of Natal thanks Cetywayo for the intelligence conveyed by his last messengers, and by the letter written at Cetywayo's request by Mr. John Dunn, dated 13th, March, 1876, and he will be glad to be informed of the occurrence of any important event in Zululand. The Lieutenant-Governor is occasionally informed by the Government of the South African Republic of events which affect its relations with the Zulus, and it is well to hear with both ears.

"The Lieutenant-Governor is fully assured that Cetywayo has been in earnest in the desire he professes, to keep the peace, and he trusts that the same desire is also felt by the Government and people of the South African Republic.

"The Government of Natal has never ceased to urge on both, the great importance of preventing a disturbance of peace of the country, because the consequences must be serious to all concerned, whatever the final issue may be.

"If, as he hopes, such a feeling exists on both sides, he does not doubt that a means will some day be found, by which all causes of difference will be adjusted without having recourse to steps that must destroy the country.

"Until that day arrives, he sincerely trusts that Cetywayo on his part will persevere in his endeavours to preserve his Country from war and keep his people from the commission

of any acts of aggressiveness that may place the relations between the Transvaal Government and himself beyond the
remedy which peaceful negotiations will afford.

" By command of His Excellency,

" (Signed)   T. SHEPSTONE,
" Secretary for Native Affairs.

" Secretary for Native Affairs Office,
" Natal, April 3rd, 1876.

" A true copy,
" J. PERRIN,
" Chief Clerk to Sec. for Native Affairs."

" *Message from His Excellency the Lieutenant-Governor of
Natal to Cetywayo, King of the Zulus, sent by Lujeli and
Umgovu.*

" It has been reported to the Lieutenant-Governor of
Natal by Gabangaye that Cetywayo intends to send two of
his sisters to be married, one to Pakade, and the other to
Gabangaye, and that he has notified such intention to these
two Chiefs.

" The Lieutenant-Governor thinks that there must be some
mistake in this, seeing that the rule of the Lieut.-Governor
being the only channel of communication between Cetywayo
and any of the Native Chiefs and people in Natal with whom
it may be necessary to communicate on any subject, has, so
far as the Lieutenant-Governor knows, never been hitherto
broken, and he has not been informed by Cetywayo of his
wish to send two of his sisters to be married to Gabangaye
and his father Pakade.

" The report having, however, been made to him, he thinks
it necessary to communicate with Cetywayo to prevent any
misunderstanding on the subject arising hereafter.

" By command of His Excellency,

"(Signed)   FRED. B. FYNNEY,

" Interpreter to the Natal Government,
for the Secretary for Native Affairs."

" Office of the Secretary for Native Affairs,
" Pietermaritzburg, May 6, 1876."

" Office of the Secretary for Native Affairs,
" 6th May, 1876.

" DEAR SIR,—The Honourable Secretary for Native
Affairs, who is at present absent with His Excellency the
Lieutenant-Governor has instructed me to send the two
messengers to deliver the enclosed message to Cetywayo.

" With a view to its being correctly delivered I beg leave
to hand it to you as it has been given to them.

" I have the honour to be,

" Dear Sir,

" Your obedient Servant,

"(Signed)   F. B. FYNNEY.

" JOHN DUNN, Esq.,
" Zululand."

" Secretary for Native Affairs Office,
        " Natal, October 3rd, 1876.

" SIR,—I transmit herewith copy of message from His
Excellency the Lieutenant-Governor of Natal to Cetywayo,
King of the Zulus, by Baiyeni and Matshonga, which will
enable you to see that it is safely delivered.

" I have the honour to be, Sir,

" Your obedient Servant,

" (Signed)   J. W. SHEPSTONE,
        " Acting Secretary for Native Affairs.

" J. L. DUNN, Zululand."

" *Message from His Excellency the Lieutenant-Governor of
Natal, to Cetywayo, King of the Zulu Country, by Bayeni
and Matshonga.*

" The Lieutenant-Governor of Natal has heard with con-
cern from various sources that many men and young women
have been lately put to death in Zululand, it is said, by order
of Cetywayo.

" The Lieutenant-Governor hopes to hear from Cetywayo
that these reports are incorrect, believing as he does that
Cetywayo remembers, and is guided by the words spoken,
and the council given to him and the Zulu Nation, by the
representative of this Government at his (Cetywayo's) installation as King.

" The Lieutenant-Governor therefore finds it difficult to
believe that such acts have taken place in Zululand, or if they

have taken place by Cetywayo's orders, he looks forward
to Cetywayo's reply in great hope of a satisfactory explanation.

"By command of His Excellency.

"(Signed)   J. W. SHEPSTONE,
"Acting Secretary for Native Affairs.

"Office of Secretary for Native Affairs,.
"Natal, 3rd October, 1876."

"Durban, 7th May, 1880.

"J. R. DUNN, Esq., Zululand.

"DEAR SIR,—I was unable to write and return your
papers until now. I am not quite clear whether you want all
back. If so, I can hardly send them through the post, and
shall be glad if you can let me know how to send them or
when you will cause a messenger to send them. In the
meantime I send what I think you particularly want—the
draft of your letter to the Aborigine's Protection Society,
Rathbone's letter, and the two from "the man who rode your
pack ox."

"I think it a great pity your letter to the A.P.S. was not
sent ; it might have prevented the war, or at all events have
prevented matters going to the extremities they did, and I
give you credit for preferring the real good of the Zulus to
any personal advantage you may have derived from the turn
things have taken. Your letter might have helped to open
the eyes of people at home to the double part Shepstone
played in the matter. I see you make no reference to the
Zulus being called up to support Shepstone's tactics with the

Boers, regarding which every now and then I see some new denial in the papers. I wish I were in a position to give the rights of this matter, and should be glad if you would give me the facts, to be used as opportunity offers.

" I think you are very probably right about the man who rode the pack ox being Harrison. I know, of course, he lived a good deal in Transvaal Territory and on the Border in these years, and think him very likely to have written the letters. But there were other Englishmen living up there who could write, and I should be glad to know what you can tell me of them, and whether they were likely to mix themselves in such matters.

" By the way, do you know anything of a man, W. Heaveride, ever living in the Zulu country?

" I hope you are getting on satisfactorily, and should be glad to hear from you from time to time. Though, for the present, I have ceased to edit the *Colonist*, my connection with the Press is not likely to be at an end, and I may still be able to do good. I am amused at the *Mercury*, which so lately was pitching into you, taking the line it now does.

" Thanks for your cheque. The account enclosed showed a small balance still at your debit. Say if you receive these letters safely.

" Yours truly,

" JOHN SANDERSON."

" *Reply of the Lieutenant-Governor of Natal to Message from the Zulu King of the 10th of November, 1878, conveyed by*

" The Lieutenant-Governor, received through Sindindi, the reply of Cetywayo to the Message of the Lieut.-Governor sent through " Umgwazi,"

" In which the Zulu King gives as his reason for assembling his army, that he had been informed that an armed body of men was being sent to the Transvaal borders, and that an armed force was to be sent into the Zulu Country to seize him.

" The Lieutenant-Governor has already informed Cetywayo that there was never was such an intention.

" Cetywayo further states that the message conveyed by Umgwazi was the first intimation he had received of the German settlers over the Pongolo being British subjects, and that Faku, the headman, did not know this. The Lieut.-Governor trusts that, now this is clear, the Zulu King and the Zulu army on the Pongolo will not again give any ground for complaint on the part of the settlers and others living on the other side of the Pongolo.

" By command of His Excellency,

" (Signed)   J. W. SHEPSTONE,
" Acting Secretary for Native Affairs.

" Secretary for Native Affairs' Office, Natal,
" December 3, 1878."

" Secretary for Native Affairs' Office,
" Pietermaritzburg, Natal,
" 4th December, 1878.

" To J. R. DUNN, Esq., Zululand.

" SIR,—I am in receipt of your letter of the 27th ult., and am directed to inform you that you are at liberty to tell Cetywayo that he need fear no invasion of his country by the

K

British Forces before the award of the Boundary question is delivered, but that after that it will all depend upon the conduct of the King as to what action the Government may take.

" The Lieut.-Governor has desired me to add that it might be well if you attended the meeting of the Envoys at the Lower Tugela, in order that you may then hear all that is said, and be able to judge for yourself as to the desirableness, or otherwise, of your leaving Zululand.

" I have the honour to be, Sir,

" Your obedient servant,

"(Signed)   J. W. SHEPSTONE,
" Acting Secretary for Native Affairs."

" Office, Secretary for Native Affairs,
" Natal, 26th December, 1878.

" To JOHN R. DUNN, Esq.

" SIR,—I have the honour to acknowledge the receipt of your letter of the 18th instant, which the Lieut.-Governor has laid before His Excellency the High Commissioner, for his information.

" I am directed to express the satisfaction of the High Commissioner at the receipt of your letter, and to inform you that the word of the Government as already given cannot now be altered.

" Unless the prisoners and cattle are given up within the time specified, Her Majesty's troops will advance ; but in consideration of the disposition expressed in your letter to comply with the demands of the Government, the troops will be halted at convenient posts within the Zulu Border, and will there await the expiration of the term of 30 days, without in the meantime taking any hostile action, unless it is provoked by the Zulus.

"(Signed)   J. W. SHEPSTONE,
"Acting Secretary for Native Affairs."

Private Message conveyed to Mr. John Dunn by two Zulu Messengers after his crossing into Natal.

"4th June, 1879.

"The King sent a word by us for your ears alone. He wishes you to ease his mind by using your influence with the great white Chiefs to get them to cease hostilities until he (the King) can hear the reason for his being destroyed. You are his father, and a child may be beaten, but let it be told why.

"Translated by me,

"F. BERNARD FYNNEY,
"Sworn Translator to the Natal Government."

Mr. John Dunn's Reply to the above.

"4th June, 1879.

"The words you bring are the same as those sent by Usitwangu. How can the King speak as he does to-day? He passed over the words I spoke to him, and cast aside my advice. I told the King—and told him with all my power on no account to fight, even although the English came into his land, but only to talk. I also told him that if the fight-
K2

ing began it would not only be for a day. I said these words
knowing the feeling of the Zulu nation, and that they did not
wish war—the King was led away by the young men. I
told him his brothers would forsake him, and that his fate
would be like that of Dingaan. Tell the King. I have no
words to send him. Matters have passed into other hands.

" (Signed)   F. BERNARD FYNNEY."

" *Conditions on which a limited number of Missionary Teachers
will be allowed to have Stations in my Territory.*

" Every Missionary desirous of being allowed to form a
Station within my Territory shall sign a deed, pledging himself to observe and carry out the following conditions :—

" 1.—He shall acknowledge my authority as Chief.

" 2.—He shall acknowledge that he has no personal claim
or title to land within the territory.

" 3.—The Schools to be established on the Mission Stations
shall be founded on the principle of an ordinary plain English
School ; both the Zulu and the English Languages being
taught, and no undue attention being given to accomplish-
ments such as music, &c.

" 4—That any native so inclinod shall be taught some
trade.

" 5.—That no native shall be allowed to remove from any
kraal to settle on a Mission Station without my consent.

" 6.—That it be distinctly understood that no native becomes exempt from his tribal duties to his Chief by residing
on a Mission Station.

" 7.—That any native desirous of residing on any Mission Station shall be bound to erect a Dwelling House in European style.

" 8.—That every encouragement be given to the cultivation by such resident natives of produce for a market.

" 9.—That the utmost encouragement be given to industrial pursuits, so as, in time, to make the Stations self-supporting.

" 10.—That the Stations shall not be allowed to be made Trading Stations for dealing in Cattle for profit.

"(Signed)   J. R. DUNN, Chief."

" Of the host of letters sent to me from all parts of the world, including South Africa, and to which I have before alluded, I select but two, as all the others were mostly applications for employment, &c., &c., and the rest uninteresting. Of course I have not the remotest idea who the person, who writes me the fellowing letter, is.

" Kilkenny, ——,

" My dear HUSBAND,—

" It is thirty long and weary years since you deserted from the 48th Regiment, leaving me young and inexperienced to drag out a long and lonely life with your son which I have done with respect to myself and with credit to your son.

" Dear John,—There was a time when I thought you could not be so hard hearted. You must know that I am, as you left me, respected by all who knows me. Though you put a blight on my young life, still the Lord in his mercy brought me through all the years we are separated, it has made no change in me but for the better, I am still Mrs. Dunne, and looks as youthful in a way as when you went

away, but I see by the papers you are married and even so I
will not ask to disturb your happiness but will live the remainder of my life bearing your name, but I would wish that
you should send me, John, some means of a living the remainder of my life, by your doing so no one shall ever hear
from me that you are my husband, and there are already
several letters come to me to know why not make my claim
now as parliament when it assembles in Februay is going to
have Bishop Colenso's letter investigated, so, dear John, I
would not give a satisfactory answer to anyone till I would
hear from you, as you did not answer your son's letter. I
trust you will mine, as my friends told me I could bring you
home under two charges, I would not wish to do so, but dear
John if I do not hear from you I must bring my case before
parliament, I have the last letter you wrote me in June, 1847,
also my two certificates of marriage and good friends to back
me.   You must know, dear John, if you were as brown as a
berry in the skin I can certify to you by that mark you bear,
your son has same and your grandchild, as your son is married
and gone to live in England. My father is dead those years
my brother Gregory died in London. Ellen died there last
May, and Catherine is married to the Quartermaster of the
50th Regiment, so that I am left the only one in Kilkenny
with my mother on my care, so dear John, I hope your letter
will be favourable, and that I will not be put to any trouble.
You can write to me, if you wish, as a sister, and I will reply
same, so that no one will ever know about you. I will now
conclude hoping you will comply, for both our sakes. When
you write, direct to—

" So-and-So,
" Kilkenny."

"P.S.—Will expect an answer by end of February.

"January 14th, 1880."

"Natal, July 20, 1881.

"To JOHN DUNN, Esq.

"DEAR SIR,—I have taking the pleasure of writen you
these few lines hoping to fine you in good health as it leaves
me the same at present thank God esquse me for writen to
you sir but my father leaves Cape Colony for some years i
leave my mother to go an look if i could fine my father and i
am two years in the transvaal and so i hear that there was
a Mr. Dunn i zulu land we are only two children what he
left i shall come to a close i reman your truly affectioned

"T. DUNN."

*Cutting from a Paper sent to me from an unknown
source.—J. L. D.*

"Whether Cetywayo, "King of the Zulus," be alive or
dead, and whether the Boers are fighting on the one side and
John Dunn on the other, are details which, in spite of their
own interest, do not affect the generally deplorable aspect of
affairs in South Africa. Every Chief in the country is now
in arms, and a civil war, which can only be ended by the
extermination after the Zulu fashion of one or other of the
contending parties, is raging. In the Western "earldoms,"
so to speak, there is a determined combination of the tribes,
who detest Cetywayo and his rule, and prefer the liberty and
the opportunities for progress that were offered them under
the scheme which Lord Wolseley inaugurated. In the
Eastern is the faction of the Monarchists, held together in the
first place by misrepresentations of British support, and in the
next by the threats of the Chiefs that all waverers in the
Royal cause will be "eaten up." How ineffectual these have
hitherto been the history of the war has abundantly shown,
for the restored King, if he be not actually dead, has been

defeated in every fight that was worth calling one. His
doughty kinsman Dabulamanzi, the bitter enemy of John
Dunn and civilisation, had mustered to the banners of the
corpulent Monarch all the old men and boys who could be
forced or coaxed into the conflict, and to these hasty levies
the terrible name of the Usutu Regiment has been given.
But the champions of popular liberty, the advocates of the
more generous régime which, until Cetywayo was restored,
seemed to be before them, thoroughly understood the composition of the impis which were brought against them, and did
not hesitate, as at Ulundi, the other day, to fall upon ten
thousand with only six hundred.   Yet these, again, are
features of the struggle having no large influence upon the
general situation, which, let the temper and composition of
the contending factions be what they may, presents itself to-
day as a striking illustration of that policy of mischievous
sentiment which, despite the warnings of all who were well
informed, persisted in accepting the vamped-up memorials for
Cetewayo's return as genuine expressions of Zulu feeling, and
which, after having given the word of the country for a
permanent settlement, withdrew it at the first invitation of
irresponsible agitators.   Never since Chaka was fighting for
the throne has Zululand been in such complete chaos, and
never since England assumed Imperial responsibilities have
her representatives faltered so weakly in their duty, or so
grievously betrayed the trust of those who confided in her.

" Yet the state of Zululand is not, after all, quite as
unworthy of British antecedents as that of Basutoland.   In
Cetewayo's territory there is this plausible excuse for failure
that we were misled into supposing the people really wanted
to have their savage ruler back again.   No treaties, except an
honourable engagement with John Dunn, stood in the way
of our doing what we considered right and profitable.   Still

with Basutoland it was very different, for we were there
bound by definite agreements to do certain things, and without any option of repudiating pledges. On three occasions
—in 1854, 1868, and 1869—we entered upon distinct engagements with the Free State and the Basutos, in the one case
to protect the Basuto border, and in the other to guarantee
the tribe against inroads from the Free State or the Colony ;
and in 1871 the Cape Government took over those engagements by the Annexation Act of that year, and accepted
responsible government. As the Basutos, however, had
grievances, and refused to put them out of sight, the Cape
Government, admitting its inability to coerce the tribe into
submission, desired to cast off its engagements ; and the
Imperial Government, while permitting it to do so, has
refused to take them again upon itself, giving, as its reason,
the repeated rebellions of the Basutos. In other words, the
British Government, having announced that it was governing
Basutoland, has committed the majority of the people to
expressions of loyalty which were resented by a turbulent and
contumacious minority. By persistence in their contumacy,
this minority has gained the day, and worn out the patience
of the British Government, which has withdrawn its protection from the loyal majority, and, while thus abandoning the
country to civil war, has left it helpless against the inroads of
its old enemies, the Boers. Of course it may be argued that,
having done our best and failed, we had no other resource
but to leave the Basutos, as we have left the Zulus, to fight
matters out among themselves. This is the doctrine of
expediency, but is it either honourable or politic ? The
Basutos, it should be remembered, were our auxiliaries
against the Zulus, and faithful allies too. We were indebted
to them, and they had claims upon our national gratitude.
Moreover, all who know them speak of them as the best of

the Kafirs ; at any rate, they are the only tribe which has
shown a general tendency to accept the institutions of
civilised administration and to conform to the requirements
of progress. They were, in fact, the single creditable out-
come of our connection with South African races, and
probably the only race that had any sympathy whatever with
us. It would, therefore, have been not unbecoming if we
had met this national desire for tranquility and advancement
half way—had insisted, by force if necessary, on the suppres-
sion of the disloyal minority, and given the Basuto people a
fair chance of prosperity. As regards the policy of abandoning them, apart from the repudiation of honourable
responsibilities, it would be difficult to contend with any
plausibility that in the present outlook of South African
affairs such an abnegation of supremacy was opportune. We
had surrendered the Transvaal because, so the Kafirs and
Boers said, we were beaten in the field. We had cancelled
the results of the Zulu war by handing back his country to
Cetewayo. And then, to round off the policy of self-depre-
ciation, we deliberately leave Basutoland to itself, because we
cannot coerce two recalcitrant members of the Royal family.
But is this good policy ? Is it statesmanship, looking forward
to the troubles which are undoubtedly in store for our
colonies, to reduce in every possible way our local prestige,
and cut off from ourselves the last possible chance of support
and alliance ? We would not go so far as some of the
members of the Cape Government, who have declared in open
Parliament that this surrender of our fair name means the
loss of South Africa in the near future. But of this the
country may be assured, that if ever the war of races to
which those speakers look forward does break out, England
in Africa will be without a friend. That such a war is not
altogether a dream may be inferred from the fact that the
Irishman Aylward, one of the staff of General Joubert during

the Transvaal War, has been lately in America with the
avowed object of obtaining materials of war 'for use against
England in the next Boer campaign.' Whether he is to be
believed or not is, of course, a question which may divide
opinion ; but he made no secret of what he was pleased to
call his 'mission from the Transvaal,' and was certainly
credited with speaking the truth by most Americans.

"It is never too late to protest against a policy which
surrenders national obligations at the bidding of force or
under apprehensions of expenditure of money, for that which
has been done here to-day may be done there to-morrow.
But as regards Zululand and the Basuto country it is, of
course, too late. There remains, however, within the space
of useful discussion the question of future procedure. With
regard to the Basutos, the point is endlessly complicated by
the neighbourhood of the Boers ; for unless we are prepared
to compel them by force to respect our wishes we must accept
the alternative, and consent to see them work their will upon
their neighbours. The Dutch farmers, it will be remembered,
are only able to exist by the employment of forced labour ; it
was the abolition of slavery among them which embittered
the Boers to exasperation against us. Independence, for
tself, was not what they sought ; it was the independence
which carried with it the power to replace Kafir slaves upon
their farms. This they have already begun to do, under Her
Majesty's suzerainty ; for the tribes of Mapoch and Mampoer,
lately conquered, have, as we were told by telegram a fort-
night or more ago, been 'indentured' out as farm hands
among the settlers of the Transvaal. Now the system of
'indenture' is that which was exposed in the Blue Books of
a few years ago as being slavery pure and simple. The
Boers, however, have not yet obtained nearly enough forced
labour for the purposes of their Republic, and every frontier

disturbance in turn will eventuate in more Kafir 'apprentices' being distributed among the farmers, and more grazing land being occupied by the aggressive Dutchmen, until the Transvaal virtually extends to the sea. Other events, moreover, that may happen are likely to give the Boers the nominal pre-eminence in South Africa which numerically they already possess ; and it is idle, therefore, to conjecture what evils may develope under British suzerainty. In Zululand, again, the presence of Cetewayo, should he be really alive, is a factor of trouble in the problem ; but, on the other hand, there can be no doubt that if matters are left to take their own course John Dunn will in the end prove too strong for the faction of Dabulamanzi. In him, a far-seeing and resolute, if self-willed, white man, Government if it chooses might perhaps find the solution of the Zulu problem, and, in strengthening his hands, fortify not only the Zulu country but Natal against any chances of successful encroachment by the Transvaal."

THE END.